KU-019-348

Sex Discrimination at Work:

A PRACTICAL GUIDE TO THE LAW IN IRELAND

John Eardly

Published in 2004 by
First Law Limited
Merchant's Court,
Merchants Quay,
Dublin 8,
Ireland.
www.firstlaw.ie

Typeset by Gough Typesetting Services, Dublin.

ISBN 1-904480-18-7

© First Law Limited

A catalogue record for this book
is available from the British Library.

4049

9200853
REF.
347.462'417
b/'04

All rights reserved. No part of this publication may be
reproduced, stored in a retrieval system or transmitted in any
form or by any means, electronic, mechanical, photocopying,
recording or otherwise, without the prior, written permission
of the publisher.

344.01'414
EAR

Printed by Johnswood Press

To my Parents and Family

PORTOBELLO COLLEGE LIBRARY
SOUTH RICHMOND STREET
DUBLIN 2.
PHONE 01-4787667

Foreword

Discrimination in the workplace has become a growing concern for all employers in Ireland. The meaning of discrimination has been broadened considerably enabling a new generation of rights to emerge. In dealing with this diverse subject of equality, John Eardly has succinctly set out the law in a clear way making an otherwise complex area of law accessible to lay people in an understanding way.

European Law has created an abundance of new legislation in Ireland and in the area of equality even more so. The increase in the number of cases coming before the Equality Tribunal bears witness to this. The forms of discrimination varies considerably from discrimination among employees, such as maternity issues, to refusing to serve drink in a public house to certain members of the community. Employers need to be more vigilant in every aspect of their work to ensure compliance with the mountain of regulations imposed by Government in the running of their businesses.

Small businesses form the backbone of Irish industry and many are too small to employ compliance officers to patrol compliance. This imposes a huge burden on Irish employers. For this reason, John Eardly's book *Sex Discrimination at Work: A Practical Guide to the Law in Ireland* is an essential book to have handy in any office. The key issues are set out in six chapters – all an employer needs to know on Sex Discrimination is contained here. To be forewarned is to be forearmed, in this instance a little knowledge is a good thing, it may save an expensive outing before a tribunal or appearance in court. Irish employers need all the practical help they can get and this book serves that purpose well.

John Eardly has to be congratulated for his knowledge of employment law and skill in imparting the information in a readable form.

Pat Delaney,
Director,
Small Firms Association,

April 28, 2004

Preface

The topic of this book concerns employment equality and sex discrimination law in Ireland. While the law and protection in this area is strong and established, it remains the case that gender inequality at work is alive and well in the modern Irish workplace. Indeed, it is an unfortunate fact that legal proceedings involving pregnancy-related discrimination remain a significant phenomenon notwithstanding thirty years of legal protection. However, what this book makes clear is that sex discrimination exists in many forms, ranging from the complexities of unequal pay to the effects of work-related victimisation and sexual harassment. It is my purpose, as author, to set out this entire range of unlawful behaviour in as practical and comprehensive a manner possible for both the layperson and lawyer alike. In doing so, I have indicated the topics, where constraints on my subject matter were necessary and desirable, on which further research might be undertaken outside the scope of this book. It has also been the aim of the author to set out the various principles, legal steps, courts and forms of redress that must be considered and navigated by litigants when dealing with claims of sex discrimination. In providing this practical advice, I have been mindful to ensure that legal claims are dealt with in this book from the perspective of both the employer and the employee and to set out, in clear language, the practical and legal ways to deal with them.

However, the readers of this book will be struck by the numerous and interwoven sources of law and legal institutions from which redress may be sought. In particular, the role of the European Union is fundamental and ever-present as the primary and most important guarantee of our freedom from gender inequality and workplace discrimination. As a result, the caselaw and legislation of the EU is specifically addressed here including the manner in which its principles have been, and continue to be, applied in Ireland. There is an onward march in the legal development of this area. While the legacy of these trends is only still emerging, it is clear that the effects of the development of equality law, both at national and EU level, will have implications far beyond the confines of the more traditional concerns relating to equal pay and treatment at work. It has been my aim to now bring together these various sources, principles, trends and institutions into one book so as to allow the reader, whether lawyer or non-lawyer, a practical and accessible guide both to the nature and scope of the protection available and to the institutions to which an employee might turn.

Finally, I would like to thank everyone who has been of assistance to me in writing this book. In particular, the author would like to thank Pat Delaney, Director of the Small Firms Association for writing the Foreword, BCM Hanby Wallace Solicitors, Dublin, Mr Roderick Horan BL, Mr Gabriel Gavigan BL and Mr Bart Daly of First Law Publications.

John Eardly,
Law Library,
Four Courts,
Dublin 7.

April 26, 2004

Table of Contents

Table of Cases

Table of Legislation

Statutory Instruments

England

Europe

Treaties

Directives

CHAPTER 1

The Meaning of Equality: An Introduction to your Rights

GENERAL OVERVIEW

We are all unique, just like everyone else?

The concept of equality has been one of the most cherished ideals of humankind. However, like all great ideals, its meaning is still elusive and open to interpretation. Whereas *inequality* festers when human differences become a source of discrimination, so too *formal equality* can also result in injustice if everyone is treated in strictly the same way despite those same differences. Therefore, the protection of equality in Ireland is not about simply replacing diversity with bland uniformity. On the contrary, it is about recognising that diversity should not become the source of arbitrary discrimination in the first place. One of the most important and direct expressions of this philosophy is contained in the Constitution of Ireland. It recognises these competing strands in our understanding of equality and provides the following important balance:

> "All citizens shall, as human persons, be held equal before the law. This shall not be held to mean that the State shall not in its enactments have due regard to differences of capacity, physical and moral, and of social function."[1]

---

1. Article 40.1, Constitution of Ireland.

The humble beginnings

This provision of the Constitution was given a narrow, literal interpretation by the courts and came to be of limited legal value to those seeking to enforce equality rights in the broader sense.[2] As a result, the primary impetus to end discrimination in Ireland only emerged following our membership of the then European Economic Community and the unavoidable obligations that this imposed.

Today, this position in Ireland has altered dramatically and is evolving. The rules against discrimination here have been supplemented in recent years by new domestic legislation that exceeds the protection afforded even by the developing European law. The Employment Equality Act 1998 and the Equal Status Act 2000 are the most important examples. These laws no longer just protect against discrimination in the work environment on the grounds of gender alone.

They also now protect against discrimination on a vastly increased number of grounds relevant to both men and women. As such, the courts and legal bodies, charged with enforcing these rules, are equally determined as never before to punish discrimination when and where it arises.

Therefore, whilst there is and continues to be much academic debate about the meaning of equality and the different sources of same, the principal purpose of this book is to offer a practical guide as to where the law now draws the line in its protection of equality and as to how one can access these rights.

---

2. *Murphy v. Attorney General* [1982] I.R. 241; *Quinn's Supermarket v. Attorney General* [1972] I.R. 1.

Chapter 2

An Equality of Rights: Economic Necessity or Constitutional Duty?

"… Respect for fundamental personal human rights is one of the greatest principles of Community law. … There can be no doubt that the elimination of discrimination based on sex forms part of those fundamental rights."[1]

Introduction

At the time of the drafting of the European Treaty of Rome, the founding Treaty of today's European Union, some Member States, such as France, already accorded a rudimentary entitlement to equal pay, through their national laws, to both genders. This equality of rights was a matter of high principle for those societies. However, it had also had a serious economic consequence. It obviously meant that the costs of production in those countries could not be reduced by the employment of more women, since the costs of their labour were pegged at the same level as their male counterparts. Other European countries, on the other hand, equally set to become Member States at that time, did indulge in gender-based discrimination in pay. As a result, they could have potentially obtained an unfair economic advantage, were

---

1. *Defrenne v. Sabena (No. 3)* [1978] E.C.R. 1365.

this inequitable industrial practice left unchecked. It was feared that they could simply engage a larger female workforce, pay them less, produce goods at a lower cost and ultimately undercut the price of goods from France where such blatant exploitation was prohibited. What was worse, in the brave new world of the Common Market, customs duties, quantitive restrictions and discriminatory internal taxation would no longer be permitted as a means of keeping the cheaper produce out.

The eventual answer to this problem arrived when it was agreed to expressly include in the Treaty of Rome, a provision ensuring equal pay for equal work and equality between men and women. As such, whether one views its inclusion as the economic self-interest of the great powers or the social concern of the liberal democracies, the effect was ultimately the same: the first piece of directly enforceable constitutional protection for women that guaranteed the equality of their economic rights, for the first time, in most of the major economies of Europe.

Economic or social policy: Where does equality fit in?

Therefore, this area of European law dealing with equality issues and the prevention of sex discrimination is known as the "Social Policy" of the Union. Although, the scope of this Policy has widened in recent years,[2] it has until recent years been primarily concerned with the equalisation of rights in both the labour market and the workplace as between the genders only as distinct from equal rights generally. As such,

---

2. *P v. S* [1996] I.R.L.R 347 (European Court of Justice). In this case, it was held that there was a breach of European law when a transexual employee was discriminated against at work as a result of gender re-assignment. This arose when the employee was treated unfavourably by comparison with persons of the gender to which he had belonged before undergoing the gender re-assignment.

discrimination on grounds unrelated to gender in the workplace had been held not to fall with the remit of European law. However, this has now changed. To this end, Council Directive 78/2000 now provides that, subject to a number of exemptions,[3] any direct or indirect discrimination based on religion or belief, disability, age or sexual orientation shall be prohibited throughout the Community. While these areas have been protected in Ireland since 1998, at the time of writing, the Oireachtas is in the process of implementing Council Directive 78/2000 by bringing our protection into line with it, through (at the time of writing) the Equality Bill 2004.

Therefore, the followings questions may be asked:

- How does European law protect us here in Ireland?

- How does Irish law and EC law interact in this area?

While a full examination of these questions is outside the remit of this book, the following is a summary of the general principles involved.

Employment equality rights today: A hierarchy of laws

European law remains the most important and ever-present protection against sex discrimination in Ireland. It exists at a level above the national law of each Member State and is superior to it. In other words, if there is a conflict between what an Irish law says, even if it is in the Constitution, and what a European law requires, the Irish law is overruled.

---

3. The two major exemptions under Council Directive 78/2000 relate, firstly, to social security and social benefit schemes whose benefits are not treated as "pay" within the meaning of Article 141 of the Treaty. The Directive is also without prejudice to national provisions laying down retirement ages. See Chap.3 below on this area in more detail.

Where any dispute arises as to what any European law means or as to whether it is being properly implemented, the ultimate arbiters are the courts of the European Union known as the Court of First Instance and the European Court of Justice. The latter court is the most important legal body of the Union. Its important role ensures uniformity of legal interpretation. The European Commission also has a quasi-judicial role although it is always subject to the aforesaid courts.

Its basic structure is not too dissimilar to the structure of the more familiar national legislation. However, because the sources of European law and the numerous institutional procedures involved in its creation are varied and complex, it will also not be dealt with in detail in this book.

Nonetheless, by way of brief summary, EC law may be understood as a body of laws essentially divided into primary and secondary rules. These are followed in turn in Ireland by implementing *national* legislation.

Level number one: Primary European Law

In the first instance, there are the primary rules derived directly from Treaties and agreed between the Member States of the Union. Treaties familiar to most are, for example, the Treaty of Rome, the Treaty of Maastricht, the Treaty of Amsterdam and the Treaty of Nice. These are then introduced into national law in accordance with the constitutional requirements of each Member State. In Ireland, this requires a referendum of the people.

Level number two: Secondary European Law

In the second instance, there is the secondary legislation passed in accordance with those Treaties that flesh out and develop their basic principles. These laws do not require a referendum but require an Act of the Oireachtas so that they can become law in Ireland. However, there are important circumstances where the rules of the European Union can be relied on directly by citizens of the Member States even where their own governments have not yet made them national law. These are known as the principles of "direct applicability" and "direct effect" and allow, when appropriate, ordinary citizens to invoke their rights under European law in their own national courts. This means that our rights under European law are not as distant as might previously be imagined. The two most important examples of secondary legislation are the **Regulations** and the **Directives** passed by either the European Council or the European Commission.

Level number three: National Law

Thirdly, these pieces of EU legislation in turn are adopted into national law in Ireland through legislation passed by the Oireachtas. In doing so, the Oireachtas must ensure that it correctly incorporates EC law entitlements into the national law of Ireland. For example, if a Directive or Regulation has been correctly incorporated into national law, there should be no need to invoke the provisions of the Directive or Regulation in order to secure the rights it accords. Where the national regime fails to correctly or at all introduce the necessary measures of European legislation into the domestic regime, or, where the manner in which it has been done is inadequate or ineffective, an Irish employee or class of employees may have no option but to seek the relief of the legal institutions of the European Union.

Moreover, national legislation implementing a European Directive or Regulation must be interpreted and applied *in light of* the wording and purpose of the Directive or Regulation. In *Nathan v. Bailey Gibson*,[4] the Supreme Court in Ireland confirmed this to be the correct approach.

---

4. [1998] 2 I.R. 162.

Moreover, in the case of *Inoue v. NBK Designs Limited*,[5] the Labour Court held, in line with the caselaw of the European Court of Justice, that the redress available to it and which it orders in any particular case, must be *effective*, *proportionate* and *dissuasive*.

As such, under the Irish regime, sex discrimination has been prohibited under several pieces of legislation incorporated to comply with our EU obligations. In particular:

(a) The Anti-Discrimination (Pay) Act 1974;

(b) The Employment Equality Act 1977;

(c) The Employment Equality Act 1998; and the

(d) The Equality Bill 2004 (passing through the Oireachtas at the time of writing).[6]

These pieces of national *primary* legislation have been the leading legislative instruments in affording redress against sex discrimination in the Irish workplace. **However, the 1998 Act has now replaced and incorporates the 1974 and 1977 Acts which have been repealed.** The earlier legislation is nonetheless still applicable to claims where the acts of discrimination complained of predate the introduction of the 1998 Act. Examples of the application of the 1974 and 1977 Acts in this way in more recent cases will be seen in the course of this book.

However, there are now also pieces of national *secondary* legislation. In particular, the *Code of Practices on Sexual*

---

5. [2003] E.L.R. 298. See also the leading case of the European Court of Justice, *Von Colson & Kamann v. Land Nordrhein-Westfalen* [1984] E.C.R. 1981.

6. Please note that the 2004 Bill is not designed as a stand-alone piece of legislation. Instead, it operates to enact amendments to the Employment Equality Act 1998 which will remain the primary Act. As such, reference will be made to this 2004 Bill where it is considered relevant to the remit of this book and where it amends the 1998 Act.

Harassment and Harassment at Work is a leading example of national secondary legislation dealing with the issue and effects of sex discrimination.[7] This Code has been in force since March 2002. It also has legal effect. This means that not only is it admissible in evidence in legal proceedings but if any provision of the code appears to be relevant to any question arising in those proceedings, it *shall* be taken into account in determining that question.[8]

Identifying discrimination: A two-pronged approach

In summary, the rules against discrimination may be divided into two categories:

I. The Rules Protecting Equal Pay, and

II. The Rules Protecting Equal Treatment.

The difference between the two is that whereas the protection of equal pay is simply concerned with the terms and scope of actual remuneration, equal treatment is concerned with the much broader issues concerning the terms and conditions of work generally, including, for example, access to employment, work-related sexual harassment, gender-related harassment and gender or pregnancy related dismissal.

The rules specifically concerning equal pay are discussed in chapter 3. The rules concerning equal treatment generally are discussed in chapters 4 and 5.

Forms of discrimination

Moreover, in legal terms, discriminatory treatment may take two forms: it may be direct or it may be indirect.

---

7. Employment Equality Act 1998 (Code of Practice) (Harassment) Order 2002 (S.I. No.78 of 2002).
8. Employment Equality Act 1998, section 56.

Direct discrimination

In sex discrimination terms, a person is directly discriminated against if he/she is paid or treated less favourably than
another is, has been or would be treated *on the grounds* of
gender. An employee may also be paid or treated differently
to others in the same or similar situation on the grounds, for
example, of marital or family status. Alternatively, an employee may be directly discriminated against when he/she is
paid or treated in exactly the same way as other employees
even though he or she is not in the same or similar situation
to those employees at all.[9]

Indirect discrimination

This form of discrimination occurs when practices or policies
that do not appear to discriminate against one group more
than another, when actually analysed more carefully, do have
a discriminatory effect. In other words, in this situation, the
difference in pay or treatment is not *on the grounds of sex*
but relates to another more neutral reason. This can happen
where a requirement, for example, which may appear on its
face to be non-discriminatory, adversely affects a particular
individual, group or class of persons more than another or
others. Moreover, indirect sex discrimination, where it is
established, can only be justified by objective factors
unrelated to *gender* This is also the case where the complaint
of sexual discrimination also includes allegations of
discrimination on the marital or family status grounds. In
other words, an employer has to undertake this exercise for
gender only and does not have to undertake the same objective
justification exercise in relation to the specific grounds of

---

9. *Gillespie v. Northern Health and Social Services Board,* European
Court of Justice, C–342/93.

family and marital status also. [10] However, before an employer is expected to objectively justify a practice or policy, the employee must have shown that he has been the subject of indirect discrimination in the first place. As we will see later in this book, this approach is adopted in both the domestic protection available in Ireland under the Employment Equality Act 1998 and EU law alike. Discrimination under Irish law is also subject to the distinction between direct and indirect discrimination.

The legal routes open in challenging sex discrimination in Ireland: How to choose?

As pointed out earlier, the legal institutions of the European Union remain paramount in enforcing and uniformly interpreting and applying the rules prohibiting sex discrimination in Ireland. However, this regime is actually implemented and supported in Ireland through a series of national structures that are in place here.

Therefore, in practical terms, in any dispute relating to sex discrimination, the majority of Irish employees are likely, depending on the circumstances, to now follow one or other of the following important statutory routes in order to challenge sex discrimination in the workplace. [11] The documentation needed to institute proceedings is largely standardised forms available from the institution to which a complainant wishes to bring his claim. [12]

---

10. See the case of *Inoue v. NBK Designs Limited* [2003] E.L.R. 98. In that Irish Labour Court case, it was determined, *inter alia*, that where a complainant makes out a *prima facie* case of indirect discrimination on the grounds of family and marital status as well as gender, the indirect discrimination nonetheless falls to be objectively justified under section 22 of the 1998 Act on the gender ground only.
11. Sections 74–93.
12. These forms are available on the various relevant websites or may

A.   The Employment Equality Act route, or

B.   The Unfair Dismissals Acts route.

A.   THE EMPLOYMENT EQUALITY ACT ROUTE

This involves challenging the complaint of sexual discrimination under the Employment Equality Act 1998.

Where to go?

1. *The Office of the Director of Equality Investigations/ Equality Tribunal (ODEI)*

Any complaint of sex discrimination (other than amounting to a claim of unfair dismissal) may be made to the ODEI/ Equality Tribunal. The Equality Tribunal may refer the claim to an **Equality Officer**, or, with the agreement of both parties, for **mediation** by an equality mediation officer. The 1998 Act provides for a specific statutory mediation service.[13]

2. *The Labour Court*

On the other hand, the Labour Court hears all claims of unfair dismissals (including constructive dismissal) arising out of

---

be obtained by contacting the institutions themselves (the Labour Relations Commission, the ODEI-Equality Tribunal or the Employment Appeals Tribunal). However, in relation to Circuit Court proceedings in this area, a Civil Bill will need to be drafted and settled in order to reflect when the specific claim is being made under the Employment Equality Act 1998 as well as, or, in the alternative to, the common law. Moreover, the parties, as well as submitting the initiating documentation will be asked to make written submissions to the Equality Tribunal and the Labour Court in advance of the hearing.

13. Sections 75(7) and 78(1), (2) and (3).

any complaint of sex discrimination under the 1998 Act. Moreover, where it appears to this court that a matter may be resolved by mediation it may also adopt this approach, if both parties are agreeable, either within its own structure or by referring it back to an equality mediation officer (as above).[14]

In a case where it is alleged that an employee was subjected to sex discrimination, a dismissal may occur in either of two ways:

i. A "direct" dismissal

This occurs where the fact of dismissal is not in dispute between the parties but there is a dispute as to the actual reasons for the dismissal and/or whether the employee was accorded fair procedures beforehand. In cases of this nature, the employee will contend that the reasons for his or her dismissal were gender-related.

ii. A "constructive" dismissal

This is where there is a dispute as to the fact of the dismissal. This situation occurs where the conditions at work become so intolerable for the employee that he or she has no option but to resign. The employer, on the other hand, may argue that the employee left of his or her own volition. As such, the employee may show that he was constructively dismissed within the meaning of the Act. There are two ways to do this.

Firstly, he or she may argue that the conduct of the employer *entitled* him or her to resign. This may occur where an

---

14. Section 77(2) and section 78(2). The Employment Appeals Tribunal has **NO JURISDICTION** to hear unfair dismissal claims made under the 1998 Act.

employer so conducts himself as to show that he does not intend to be bound by the contract of employment. In cases of this nature, the Labour Court will have regard to the nature of the employment relationship between the parties and to those requirements essential to all employment agreements, in particular, the need for mutual trust and confidence in the workplace.[15]

Secondly, even if an employee cannot show his or her entitlement to resign, he or she will ask the Labour Court to look at the surrounding circumstances and conclude that it was *reasonable* for him or her to do so. A claim of constructive dismissal may not necessarily be defeated where the employee does not give any reasons for her resignation or where the reasons given when challenging the dismissal are different to those given when the employee resigned. The law accepts that there may be important reasons why an employee may not want to record her actual intolerance of the workplace at the time she has to resign and that this should not automatically damage a claimant's credibility. One example is where the employee may fear a real detriment such as being refused a reference. Factors such as these may only become apparent at the conclusion of all the evidence at a hearing and therefore the courts and tribunal prefer to proceed rather than unfairly write off what might be a valid claim.

However, in certain cases, an employee may fail in a claim of constructive dismissal on the basis that the action he took by resigning, without recourse to a grievance procedure, was precipitous.

3. *The Circuit Court*

In **all** claims on the gender ground relating to sex discrimi-

---

15. The same principles will apply in relation to claims for constructive dismissal under the Unfair Dismissals Acts 1977–2001.

nation (up to and including an unfair dismissal), the employee may bypass the above two bodies and refer the matter directly to the appropriate Circuit Court.[16]

The circuit in which the claim is brought must be the one covering the geographic area where the employer resides or carries on any business, profession or occupation.[17]

4. *Parallel claims: Complaints to the Equality Tribunal and the Labour Court*

Finally, it appears that a claimant may now also have a two-fold cause of action. Where, for example, an employee has been the subject of an extended period of unchecked work-related sex discrimination (such as sexual harassment) that ultimately provokes him or her to resign, he or she may now institute proceedings before the Equality Tribunal for compensation for the incidents of sex discrimination suffered in this way prior to resignation, **and** also proceedings before the Labour Court for compensation for the unfair dismissal when she ultimately resigned.[18]

This approach initially appeared to suffer from the risk of potentially falling "between two stools". In other words, what happened to a claim against a discriminatory and unfair dismissal in the Labour Court, if the Equality Tribunal, beforehand, having heard a parallel claim, not for dismissal but for sexual discrimination *leading up to the dismissal* arising from the same facts, finds against the claimant in all or any aspect of this sex discrimination claim? Is he or she then stuck with the findings of the Equality Tribunal going into his or her new and separate claim for the unfair dismissal

---

16. Section 77(3).
17. Section 80(2).
18. *A Complainant v. A Company* [2002] E.L.R. 230; *O'Hanlon v. Educational Building Society* [2002] E.L.R. 107.

before the Labour Court? An answer to this question is found
in the case of *New Era Packaging v. A Worker*.[19]

Background In this case, the claimant had commenced
employment with the respondent company on November 27,
1989 and ceased work on December 19, 1997. She claimed
that she had been the focus of sexual harassment by various
male members of staff. She further alleged that she had been
forced to work on a daily basis in an environment that was
abusive and characterised by sexually offensive remarks and
innuendo. She claimed as a result she had no option but to
resign her post.

However, arising out of the same allegations, the claimant
also referred a complaint relating her subjection to
discriminatory working conditions which was heard by an
Equality Officer of the Equality Tribunal. The Equality
Officer determined that in respect of all but one of the
incidents of alleged sexual harassment, the claimant had not
made out her case. In respect of one ground of alleged sex
dis-crimination, she was awarded **£3,000**.

Therefore, in the claim for unfair dismissal in the Labour
Court, the respondent argued that the claimant was now bound
by the findings of fact made by the Equality Officer in his
earlier investigation and should not be entitled to adduce
evidence in her Labour Court claim which contradicted those
findings.

The claimant argued that she was not prevented
("estopped") from relying in the Labour Court on the incidents
to which the evidence before the Equality Officer also related.

Findings The Labour Court concluded that the claimant was
not estopped from relying on her evidence before the Equality
Officer.

Firstly, this did not prejudice the respondent.

19. [2001] E.L.R. 122.

Secondly, it determined that even if the findings of the Equality Officer had a legally binding effect, which they do not, the previous complaint arose in relation to discriminatory work conditions, whereas the present case was in relation to a dismissal. In the circumstances, the Labour Court was satisfied that the claimant was not bound in the Labour Court in her case for dismissal on the findings of fact made by the Equality Officer.

Finally, the Labour Court was satisfied that the claimant had been recurrently subjected to sexual harassment by her male colleagues and that the respondent, when it knew or ought to have known that this was recurring, failed in its duty of care to her. As a result, she was reasonably entitled to treat her contract of employment as repudiated by her employer. As such, she was awarded **£5,000** in compensation for the dismissal by the Labour Court.

How long do you have to make a complaint under the 1998 Act?

Time limits A complaint must be referred to the ODEI-Equality Tribunal, the Labour Court or to the Circuit Court within six months of the alleged incident of discrimination or of the latest incident of such act(s) of discrimination to which the claim relates. This may be extended to up to 12 months where exceptional circumstances prevented the making of the complaint within the original six months.[20] In the case of a claim to the Circuit Court under the 1998 Act, the normal limitation period of six years for breach of employment contract cases does **not** apply. Moreover, where a delay in referring a case under this Act to the Director, Labour Court or Circuit Court is attributable to the respondent employer misrepresenting to an employee the facts, upon

---

20. Section 77(6).

which his or her case depends, the date of referral by which a complaint should be made shall relate in the future not to the date of discrimination but to the date of mis-representation.[21]

Compensation The maximum amount that can be awarded by either the Office of the Director of Equality Investigations or by the Labour Court is 104 weeks remuneration as received or, where it is greater, 104 weeks remuneration that the employee would have received had there not been any discrimination or victimisation in the workplace.[22] The 1998 Act also expressly provides that enactments relating to the jurisdiction of the Circuit Court are not to be taken as limiting the amount of compensation that may be awarded by that Court in claims under the 1998 Act.[23] This means that the normal jurisdictional limit of the Circuit Court, namely €38,000 (£30,000), is not applicable. In terms of compensation, this is the most serious situation an employer may, therefore, find himself in.

Reinstatement or re-engagement In the event of a dismissal, the Labour Court or the Circuit Court may order a reinstatement or a re-engagement, with or without compensation, as appropriate.[24] The Circuit Court will primarily come into contact with a dismissal claim under the 1998 Act either at first instance when the discriminatory dismissal is alleged to be on the grounds of gender or on appeal from a decision of the Labour Court.

Equal treatment or other specified course of action Section 82 of the 1998 Act also provides that redress may

---

21. Section 33(9) of the Equality Bill 2004 (At time of writing, passing through the Oireachtas).
22. Section 82(4).
23. Section 82(3).
24. Section 82(2) and section 82(3).

take the form of a specified course of action to remedy the discrimination complained of. What these may be will depend on the circumstances of each individual case.[25]

Right of appeal

From Director/Equality Tribunal to Labour Court The decision of an Equality Officer (under the rubric of the ODEI-Equality Tribunal) may be appealed by either the respondent or the applicant not later than 42 days **from *the date* of the decision** by notice in writing to the Labour Court specifying the grounds of appeal. In course of hearing that appeal, the Labour Court may refer a point of law to the High Court and adjourn the appeal pending an answer.[26]

Under the route where a claimant starts out *at first instance* before an Equality Officer, no further appeal will lie to the Circuit Court. A further appeal would only then lie to the Supreme Court from the High Court on its point of law judgment. In terms of procedurally making an appeal on a point of law to the High Court from the Labour Court, it appears, in the absence of concrete rules of court on the point, any such appeals or references to the High Court on a point of law should be effected by way of special summons by analogy with Orders 105 and 106 of the Rules of the Superior Courts 1986. As such, this type of appeal must be lodged within 21 days of the date of determination of the Labour Court (although there is provision in the Orders for this to be extended to 42 days in exceptional circumstances).[27]

From Labour Court to Circuit Court Where the claim relates to an unfair dismissal before the Labour Court *at first*

---

25. Section 82(1)(d) and (e).
26. Section 83(1) and section 90(4).
27. Kerr, Anthony, *Employment Equality Legislation*, Section 30 Annotation, (2001, Dublin, Roundhall Sweet & Maxwell).

instance, the decision of the Labour Court may be appealed
to the Circuit Court by either party not later than 42 days
from *the date* of the determination of the Labour Court or
such further time as the Circuit Court may allow. In this
situation, you start your complaint in the Labour Court unlike
above where it starts in the Equality Tribunal. The decision
of the Circuit Court is final and conclusive. However, this is
subject to an appeal by either party to the High Court on a
point of law only.[28]

Judicial review? It is important to remember that an appeal
is different from a judicial review. Essentially, judicial review
arises where a claimant or respondent is advised that the
decision of a statutory body is so fundamentally wrong that
it cannot or ought not be remedied by appeal and must instead
be set aside altogether by the High Court (or the Supreme
Court on appeal). As a statutory body with quasi-judicial
powers both the Equality Tribunal and the Labour Court are
at all times amenable to judicial review. However, the extent
of the discretion vested in these bodies, particularly the
Labour Court, is very broad. This was recently confirmed in
respect of the Labour Court in the case of *Mulcahy v.
Waterford Leadership Partnership*,[29] where O'Sullivan J. of
the High Court held:

> "… the Court is rejecting the invitation to draw
> an inference [and to again consider] all the
> material including the oral evidence and the
> cross-examination. That is precisely the dis-
> cretionary quasi-judicial function with which the
> Labour Court (and no one else) is charged to
> carry out. The fact that one may disagree with
> the conclusion, or strongly disagree with it is –

28. Section 90(1) and (2).
29. [2002] E.L.R. 12.

in law – neither here nor there. It is the Labour Court and no one else which is charged under our law with carrying out this quasi-judicial function and it is only if their conclusion is so abhorrent to logic and common sense or involves an error of law that the High Court will interfere with it."[30]

How decisions and settlements are enforced by the law

Where the employer fails to comply with a **final determination of the Equality Tribunal or the Labour Court** an application can be brought by the employee to the Circuit Court and it shall make an order directing the carrying out of the decision of either the Office of the Director of Equality Investigations, Equality Tribunal or the Labour Court in accordance with its terms. This application cannot be made before the time allowed to appeal the decision has expired (namely, 42 days).[31]

Where the parties agree to **a mediated settlement** of a claim and one of the parties has failed to give effect to the terms of the settlement, in whole or in part, then an application can be brought to the Circuit Court and it shall make an order directing the carrying out of the settlement in its entirety. However, the Circuit Court cannot enforce any aspect of this mediated settlement agreed between the parties that could not have been provided as a relief under the 1998 Act. This application cannot be made before the expiry of 42 days from the date of the written record of the settlement.[32]

The Circuit Court, when asked to enforce a decision or

---

30. See also the High Court case of *Thompson v. Tesco Ireland* [2002] E.L.R. 21 *per* Lavan J.
31. Section 91(1) and (3).
32. Section 91(2) and (4).

mediated settlement in this way, can actually make **additional orders** to punish an employer for failing to comply.[33]

This court can also, where it considers appropriate, make an order **substituting the earlier decision** of an Equality Officer or of the Labour Court to re-engage or reinstate an employee for an order of compensation instead. The maximum compensation that may be awarded in this way *in lieu of reinstatement or re-engagement* is calculated on the same basis as provided above.[34]

Criminal conviction

An employer may also be criminally convicted under the 1998 Act. He or she may be prosecuted summarily by a Court Judge or on indictment before a jury. On conviction, he may be fined or imprisoned or both.[35]

Two offences draw the serious implications of a criminal prosecution under the 1998 Act. Firstly, if an employee dismisses an employee for seeking relief or otherwise relying on his entitlements under the Act. This is known as *'victimisation'* and is dealt with below. Victimisation may also be dealt with under civil sanctions. Secondly, an employer who obstructs or impedes the Labour Court, the Office of the Director or one of its Equality Officers or otherwise fails to comply with one of their requirements in the course of the proceedings is also guilty of a criminal offence and is at risk of prosecution.[36]

As well as the Act, the failure of an employer to comply with an order of the Circuit Court is contempt of court and may result in **imprisonment**.

---

33. Section 92.
34. Section 93.
35. Section 100.
36. Section 98(1) and (8).

B. THE UNFAIR DISMISSALS ROUTE

If a complaint of sex discrimination relates to challenging, in particular, a gender or pregnancy-related dismissal, a claim may be brought under the Unfair Dismissals Acts 1977 to 2001. This is similar to the Employment Equality Act 1998 route as above in that it covers direct and constructive dismissals also.[37] However, unlike the Employment Equality Act 1998, which is limited to only nine grounds of discrimination prescribed therein (including gender, marital and family status), the Unfair Dismissals Acts route is not so limited and may be used to challenge a dismissal on the grounds of unfairness generally. However, an employee cannot proceed on **both** the Employment Equality Act and the Unfair Dismissal Acts route in order to challenge the same dismissal. He/she must choose between them. For example, an employee may choose the unfair dismissal here route here where he or she feels or is advised that there is a risk that they do not have sufficient evidence (despite their suspicions) to prove that their dismissal was motivated by sex discrimination *per se* in which case there is a risk that he/she will fall outside the remit of the Employment Equality Act 1998.

Therefore, if an employee chooses to challenge a dismissal using the Unfair Dismissals Acts, the following issues are relevant.

---

37. See *Browne v. Ventelo Limited*, UD 507/2001, July 16, 2002. In that sexual harassment-related case before the EAT, the claimant had filled out a form before she left recording her reasons for leaving as "travelling." This was held not to undermine her credibility for a constructive dismissal claim in light of all the other circumstances of her case.

Where to go?

1. At first instance: Rights' Commissioner or Employment Appeals Tribunal?

The claim may be heard at first instance before either **a Rights' Commissioner** or **the Employment Appeals Tribunal** ("EAT"). The Rights Commissioner Service and the EAT are independent bodies bound to act judicially between the parties.[38] However, if either party objects to having a claim heard before a Rights' Commissioner it must proceed to the EAT for hearing at first instance.[39]

2. On appeal: Employment Appeals Tribunal or Circuit Court?

If a claim proceeds at first instance to a Rights' Commissioner, then either party to the dispute has a right of appeal to the Employment Appeals Tribunal. This appeal must be brought within six weeks of the *date of the deter-mination*.[40]

If the claim proceeds to the EAT at first instance, then either party may appeal to the Circuit Court within six weeks of the date of the determination of the EAT.[41] The appropriate Circuit Court to hear the appeal is the one in which the employer ordinarily resides or carries on his profession, trade or business.

3. Judicial Review?

In very limited circumstances, there may be a case to be made for a judicial review of a decision of the Employment Appeals Tribunal (or very extremely and unusually, the Rights'

---

38. Section 8(1) of the Unfair Dismissals Act 1977 (as amended).
39. Section 8(3) of the 1977 Act.
40. Section 9 of the 1977 Act.
41. Section 10(4) of the 1977 Act.

Commissioner). However, the principles, caselaw and issues as discussed above in relation to judicially reviewing the Labour Court would similarly apply here.

4. Circuit Court enforcement procedure

Where an employer does not appeal, but fails to comply with a determination of the Rights' Commissioner or EAT at first instance, then the claimant may apply to the Minister for Enterprise and Employment to, in turn, apply on behalf of the employee to the Circuit Court in order to enforce same. The Minister in doing so and in satisfying the Court that the employee is entitled to the relief claimed, can also apply for and be awarded an order for legal costs against the employer for having to make the application in question.[42] Similarly, the employee can make the application himself.

What do you have to show in an unfair dismissals claim?

Under the Unfair Dismissals Acts, a complainant must lodge his or her unfair dismissal claim with the offices of the EAT within six months from the date of dismissal. This may be extended to 12 months from the date of dismissal in exceptional circumstances.[43]

The 1977 Act provides that a dismissal is unfair unless there are substantial grounds in order to justify it. As such, in a claim of this nature, where there is a "direct" dismissal, the burden of proof rests with the employer to show that the dismissal he or she has effected was fair and that there were substantial grounds justifying it.[44] However, where the dismissal is in dispute, namely, a constructive dismissal, the

---

42. Section 10(1) of the 1977 Act.
43. Section 8(2) of the 1977 Act.
44. Section 6(1) of the 1977 Act. Examples of substantial grounds

burden of proof rests with the employee to show that a dismissal rather than a voluntary resignation occurred. In the event that the employee succeeds in doing this, then the burden again shifts back to the employer as above to show that the dismissal was fair.

In particular, a dismissal shall be deemed to be unfair if it results wholly or mainly from the pregnancy of the employee or matters connected therewith unless:

1. The employee was unable to do the work for which she was employed **or** she could not have continued to do so without breaching statute; **and**

2. There was not at the time of the dismissal any suitable employment available for her at work in relation to which there was a vacancy; **or**

3. She refused an offer of alternative employment made to her for a job with corresponding terms and conditions as the one from which she was dismissed so as to enable her to be retained in the employment of the employer.[45]

What redress is available?

Under the Unfair Dismissals Acts 1977–2001, the three options for redress are reinstatement, re-engagement or compensation.

Reinstatement means being restored to the actual position held immediately prior to the dismissal.

Re-engagement means being restored to employment with the same employer, but not necessarily to the same position prior to being dismissed.

Compensation is based on the financial loss attributable

---

that justify a dismissal are the competence of an employee, his qualifications, his continued capability to do the job for which he was employed and his conduct.

45. Section 6(2)(f) of the 1977 Act (as amended).

to the dismissal as is just and equitable in all the circumstances. In deciding what is just and equitable, the EAT can look to any acts or omissions of the parties that contributed to the dismissal and can look at the reasonableness of the employer. For example, in dismissing the employee, did the employer apply or deviate from his or her own disciplinary procedures or any relevant Code of Practice. Moreover, financial loss is divided between actual loss and prospective loss. Actual loss is the loss of earnings suffered during the period in which the dismissed employee was out of work seeking alternative employment. Prospective loss relates to any disparity in income that the employee may now suffer because his or her new job is not as well paid as the one from which they were dismissed. However, there is a cap on the maximum amount of compensation that may be awarded to a claimant for an unfair dismissal. It cannot exceed 104 weeks gross remuneration for the job from which he or she was dismissed. Since 1993, even where an employee can show no financial loss attributable to the dismissal, the EAT has still now a discretion to award compensation equal to four weeks remuneration at the most.[46]

Exclusions?

Before an employee can rely on the Unfair Dismissals Acts 1977–2001, he or she must be an employee (as distinct from a self-employed/independent contractor) and must also overcome a number of jurisdictional obstacles and exclusions.[47]

However, while an employee must normally have had *at least* **one year's continuous service** before he or she can take a claim, *this does not apply to the area of pregnancy related dismissals under the Act.*

---

46. See section 7 of the 1977 Act (as amended).
47. Sections 2–5 of the 1977 Act (as amended).

On the other hand, the 1977–2001 Acts, by definition, can only apply once matters have reached the point of an alleged dismissal having occurred, whether constructive or direct. As such, the Unfair Dismissal Acts' route does not, unlike the Employment Equality Act 1998, permit redress or for the intervention of outside agencies internally in the workplace until this point of dismissal has been reached. If an employee does not have a complaint about a dismissal, this route is therefore of no use to him or her.

C. OTHER POSSIBLE ROUTES

Finally, as well as or in the alternative to the above, in practice, there may be a number of other available routes to an employee who wishes to challenge incidents of sex discrimination. However, specific legal advice should always be taken as to whether such other routes are available or applicable in any particular case. These other claims, *inter alia*, may relate to:

> i. The Industrial Relations Acts 1946–2001;
> ii. A civil action claim for wrongful dismissal. This type of claim is an alternative to the statutory claims for unfair dismissals as set out above. If successful at the hearing of the case, the employee will be awarded damages for his loss as a result of the breach of contract. This is calculated on the basis of his actual loss and does not relate to compensation for distress or upset suffered as a result of the breach.[48] Where an employee wishes to challenge his dismissal in this way, he also has the facility to seek an

---

48. *Addis v. Gramophone Company Limited* [1909] A.C. 488 (England).

injunction before the civil courts restraining the alleged breach of his contract of employment (namely the dismissal) and maintaining the *status quo* pending the substantive trial of the dispute. This facility is not available under the statutory route of unfair dismissal. An injunction of this nature may be granted pending the full hearing of a case in circumstances where damages would *not* be an adequate remedy were the injunction not granted. This is known as an interlocutory injunction. In order to get such an injunction, an employee must show that there is a fair issue to be tried between the parties and he must give an undertaking as to damages to his employer. This means that he agrees to compensate the injuncted employer in the event that the claim is unsuccessful and where the injunction has caused the employer loss. The court then decides, at its entire discretion and on a balance of convenience between the parties, whether to grant such an injunction. An injunction may also form part of a final order made against an employer at the end of the entire proceedings. This is called a perpetual injunction. However, these are quite rare.

A civil action claim for damages for a personal injury
Where the health of an employee, either physical or mental, is damaged as a result of being subject over a period of time to conduct also amounting to sex discrimination (for example, serious sexual harassment), an employee may be able to proceed with a personal injury civil action *in addition to* an wrongful/unfair dismissal action.

Judicial review proceedings where an employee works in the public/civil service This is different to the judicial review discussed earlier which related to reviewing the statutory employment tribunals themselves. In the context here, an employee may wish to initiate judicial review proceedings against his public/civil service employer from the outset in order to challenge a decision made in relation to his terms and conditions of employment and/or the absence of fair procedures in relation to same.

Employment equality and the burden of proof

Therefore, in light of the various routes available to *challenge* sex discrimination, what do you actually have to do to *prove* sex discrimination?

The answer to this question is primarily found under an important piece of legislation entitled the Burden of Proof Directive 97/80.[49] This provides that the burden of proof dealing with discrimination on the grounds of gender, lies firstly with the employee.[50] However, it then shifts to the impugned employer when the complaining employee establishes:

> "facts from which it may be presumed that there
> has been direct or indirect gender discrimination
> in relation to him or her."

This is known as the "*prima facie*" burden of proof. This burden of proof is now also applicable under Irish law to the gender and other grounds of discrimination under the Employment Equality Act 1998. In other words, if an employee is alleging direct or indirect discrimination on the

---

49. Implemented into Irish law by the EC (Burden of Proof in Gender Discrimination Cases) Regulations 2001 (S.I. No. 337 of 2001).
50. Interestingly, the burden of proof required under the Unfair Dismissals Acts 1977–2001 is more onerous in that the burden remains on an employer (except in constructive dismissal claims) at all times to show that the dismissal was fair.

grounds, for example, of gender, marital status or family status then the burden of proof remains the same as if he or she were making a claim specifically for gender discrimination.[51]

In *Hughes v. Aer Lingus*,[52] the following summary of the current approach was made:

> "It is now established practice of Equality Officers, in relation to the burden of proof in non-gender discrimination complaints that under the 1998 Act, to follow the traditional approach of Equality Officers and of the Labour Court in relation to the gender and marital status grounds, of shifting the burden of proof when the complainant has established a *prima facie* case. This is essentially the same practice as that subsequently applied by the European Court of Justice (in gender cases only). ... It is for the complainant to establish at first instance as fact, one or more of the assertions on which the complaint is based, and, having thus established a *prima facie* case, the burden of proof rests with the respondent to demonstrate that discrimination did not take place."

However, in practice, where to draw the line can be difficult. For example, it must be borne in mind that both the Equality Tribunal and the Labour Court must be satisfied that the conduct complained of is not simply unfair, it must *also* be conduct that allows an inference of discrimination to be drawn under the Employment Equality Act 1998. This is a very

---

51. See the following cases, *Sheehan v. DPP*, DEC–E2002–047; *An Employee v. A Government Department*, DEC–E2002–056; *Margetts v. Graham Anthony & Co. Limited*, DEC–E2002–050 and *Hughes v. Aer Lingus*, DEC–E2002–049.

52. DEC–E2002–049.

important consideration for both lawyers and complainants alike since their prospects of showing that the unlawful conduct was discriminatory as well as unfair has a vital bearing on deciding what route to take in challenging that conduct. If there is significant doubt that the complainant, despite his or her suspicions, can show *prima facie* that they have been discriminated against as well as treated unfairly, or, if the discrimination relates to a ground not covered by the 1998 Act, then it may be appropriate to institute proceedings under one of the other pieces of employment legislation.[53]

In *Mitchell v. Southern Health Board*,[54] the Labour Court in a gender discrimination claim set out the manner in which a complainant must discharge the burden of proof for sex discrimination. In particular, it determined that the complainant:

> "… must prove, on the balance of probabilities, the primary facts upon which they rely in seeking to raise the presumption of unlawful discrimination. It is only if those primary facts are regarded by the Court as being of sufficient significance to raise a presumption of discrimination that the onus shifts to the respondent to prove that there was no infringement of the principle of equal treatment."

This principle is now extensively applied to all the grounds of discrimination such as family and martial status by the

---

53. See the decision of the Labour Court in *Mulcahy v. Waterford Leader Partnership*, EEO 1/00 wherein it was held that unfairness on the part of an employer may not *in itself* be evidence of discrimination. In such circumstances where a claim relates to unfairness rather than discrimination, see the Unfair Dismissals Acts 1977–2001; Industrial Relations Acts 1946–2001.
54. [2001] E.L.R. 201.

Equality Tribunal and Labour Court alike in a claim under the 1998 Act.

The "primary facts" criteria to establish *prima facie* discrimination were defined in a recent discrimination case by an Equality Officer of the Equality Tribunal:[55]

> "It appears to me that the three key elements which need to be established by a complainant in order to show that a *prima facie* case exist are:
>
> i.   that he/she is covered by the relevant discriminatory ground(s);
> ii. that he/she has been subject to specific treatment, and;
> iii. that this treatment is less favourable than the way someone who is not covered by the discriminatory ground is, has been or would be treated."[56]

In *Davis v. Dublin Institute of Technology*,[57] Quirke J. further confirmed that:

> "In cases where discrimination on grounds of sex is alleged to have occurred contrary to the provisions of section 2(a) of the 1977 Act, the fact that there is a gender difference between the successful and unsuccessful applicants for a post or for promotion does not, by itself require Tribunals such as the Labour Court to look for an explanation. ... A primary finding of fact by such a tribunal of discrimination, or, of a significant difference between the qualifications

---

55. *Minaguchi v. Winesport Lakeshore Restaurant*, DEC–E2002–020.
56. Unreported, High Court, June 23, 2000.

> of a candidate '*together with*' a gender difference
> may give rise to such a requirement. ..."

Therefore, the mere fact that the complainant and the successful candidate are of different genders will not be enough to shift the burden of proof to the respondent. However, the burden of proof may shift where the complainant is of a different gender under the 1998 Act (gender, family or marital status) *and* appears to be objectively better qualified, according to the job criteria fixed by the respondent. In such a case, the respondent may be required to show that the difference in treatment is not discriminatory.

How this is approached may be discerned from the following case, *McGinn v. The Daughters of Charity of St Vincent de Paul.*[57]

When "unfairness" becomes "discrimination"?

Background The complainant was employed by the respondent as a registered nurse for the mentally disabled. In August 2001, the post of Nurse Practice Development Co-ordinator with the respondent became temporarily vacant. The complainant was one of two candidates for the post. The other candidate was a male nurse employed by the respondent. In the subsequent competition, the male candidate was successful. The complainant alleged that she had been discriminated against in the filling of this post contrary to section 6(2)(a) and section 8 of the 1998 Act. The claimant also alleged that she had been victimised by her employer under section 4 of the 1998 Act when she sought to pursue her grievance about her failure to be appointed to the post. Her complaint was:

---

57. Decision of the Labour Court, August 12, 2003.

    i. She was better qualified academically than the successful candidate;

   ii. The essential qualification for the post at issue, five years post registration experience, was deviated from in the case of the successful male candidate;

  iii. The marking at interview did not reflect the complainant's greater qualifications and experience;

  iv. The successful male candidate had been advised by a member of management to apply for the post, and that this manager was subsequently a member of the interview panel for the post;

   v. The post was internally advertised despite the fact that it had indicated that it would be advertised in the public press.

  vi. The manner in which her interview was conducted was unsatisfactory in comparison to that of the male candidate. In particular, she was not questioned about relevant issues concerning her career, and the questions put to her did not permit a direct answer on her part. Moreover, the atmosphere at the interview was uncomfortable in comparison to the successful candidate who was escorted out of the interview room in cordial circumstances.

  vii. The interview board did not keep notes of the interview.

The respondent denied the allegations. The respondent contended that there was no evidence of any bias against the appointment of women to managerial posts in its institution. In fact, the evidence pointed to the contrary conclusion. Moreover, the interview board was made up of three women and this would normally be regarded as having the potential to confer an advantage on women candidates. There was also no suggestion that any of the questions asked of the complainant at the interview inferred any discriminatory disposition on the part of any member of the interview board.

Therefore, the respondent contended that the allegations of the complainant, even if there were deficiencies, at the very worst, only supported an inference of *unfairness* (which it denied), but **not** of discrimination.

At first instance, the Equality Tribunal, it found in favour of the complainant and she was awarded €70,000 overall for the discrimination. This was divided into €60,000 for arrears of remuneration and €10,000 for the stress suffered as a result of the discrimination. The respondent appealed to the Labour Court.

Findings The Labour Court rejected the proposition that *unfairness* can never be an acceptable basis on which to shift the burden of proof on the respondent. However, it held that it was a matter of degree, and it was for the Tribunal or Court to decide in every case if the factual basis disclosed on the evidence was sufficient *to raise an inference of discrimination* arising from that unfairness.

Therefore, where, in circumstances such as here, there was unfairness in a selection process which disadvantaged a woman candidate to the advantage of a man, an inference on the gender ground will properly follow.

This conclusion may appear at first sight to come very close to the risk identified by Mr Justice Quirke above in *Davis*, that gender difference alone should not raise an inference of discrimination. However, the reasoning of the Labour Court made clear that this was not the case.

As such, in assessing the evidence and in concluding whether, as well as unfairness, an inference of discrimination could be drawn, the Labour Court stated that the case for such a finding was finely balanced here.

Firstly, the Labour Court also had regard here to the earlier Northern Ireland decision of *Wallace v. South Eastern Education and Library Board*,[58] where it was held that if the successful candidate was male and the other more qualified unsuccessful candidate was female, then this is, in itself, evidence of gender discrimination.

Secondly, in concluding that this inference could be drawn, it looked to the following factors:

   i. The respondent had deviated from its selection criteria and even its original job advertisement in this particular case.

   ii. The respondent attached equal weight to the educational qualifications of the candidates even though the complainant's educational qualifications were greater and complied with the recommendations of the Department of Health and Children.

   iii. There were no notes taken at the interview and the individual board members did not mark the candidates. Comments were also added by them about the candidates to an assessment form but there was no documentary basis for those comments.

   iv. Although the complainant scored highly for the post, she was designated as not suitable for the post rather than being listed as a reserve candidate.

As such, the Labour Court found that these factors were of sufficient significance so as to raise a presumption of discrimination as required under the Burden of Proof Directive 97/80. As such, the onus of proving that the principle of equal

58. [1980] I.L.R.M 193 *per* Lord Lowry L.C.J.

treatment had not been infringed rested with the respondent. They failed to do so.

Conclusions The Labour Court concluded that the complainant had been discriminated against on the grounds of her gender. However, in relation to her complaint that she was subsequently victimised for complaining, the court concluded against her, the Labour Court reduced the amount of compensation to be paid to the Complainant to **€25,000**.

As such, having assessed, in this chapter, the **general principles** that apply to the area of sex discrimination, including the legal routes available to challenge sex discrimination and the principles that apply, in the following chapter, one of the fundamental cornerstones of the prohibition against sex discrimination is set out and discussed, namely, the right to equal pay.

CHAPTER 3

Equal Pay: Inequality of Pay – The Enduring Legacy of Workplace Discrimination

"It is settled law that discrimination can only arise through the application of different rules to comparable situations or the application of the same rules to different situations."[1]

GENERAL OVERVIEW

As referred to earlier, European law may be divided between primary and secondary laws. The rules on equal pay are no exception.

The Treaty: Primary law

The primary law on Equal Pay is found in Article 141 (formerly Article 119) of the European Community Treaty (ECT). This provides that:

1. Each Member State shall ensure that the principle of equal pay for male and female workers for:

   i. Equal work; **or**
   ii. Work of *equal value* is applied.

---

1. *Finanzamt Koein-Alstadt v. Schumacker* [1995] E.C.R. I–225.

2. For the purposes of this Article, "pay" means the ordinary, basic or minimum wage or salary and any other consideration, whether in cash or in kind, which the worker receives, directly or indirectly, in respect of his employment from his employer.

3. Equal pay without discrimination based on sex means:
    (a) that pay for the same work at piece rates shall be calculated on the basis of the same unit of measurement;
    (b) that pay for work at time rates shall be the same for the same job;

4. The Council, acting in accordance with the procedures referred to in Article 251, and after consulting the Economic and Social Committee, *shall adopt measures to ensure the application of the principle of equal opportunities and equal treatment of men and women in matters of employment and occupation, including the principle of equal pay for equal work or for work of equal value.*

5. With a view to ensuring full equality in practice between men and women in working life, the principle of equal treatment shall not prevent any Member State from maintaining or adopting measures providing for specific advantages in order to make it easier for the under-represented sex to pursue a vocational activity or to prevent or compensate for disadvantages in professional careers.

All employees and employers covered

The above rules on equal pay vest directly in each individual employee and apply to all employers. In those circumstances, the national courts and tribunals in Ireland *have an overriding duty* to ensure the protection of those rights for employees.

An employee may enforce the principle of equal pay for equal work or work of equal value whether employed by a <u>public body</u> or a <u>private party</u>[2]. It is also enforceable as against discriminatory provisions in <u>collective agreements</u>.[3]

When a violation of Article 141 is established in a collective agreement, the national court must disapply the offending provision and extend to the victims of discrimination the same arrangements as applied to the other employees. There is no need to await a collective renegotiation.[4]

However, there is one slight limitation to the enforceability in national courts of Article 141 that should not be forgotten by employers, employees or their lawyers alike. This relates to the distinction in Article 141 between the criterion of "equal work" and that of "work of equal value."

"Equal work"

Article 141 (formerly Article 119) *is* directly effective where the discrimination complained of is simply a breach of **the equal pay for equal work** criterion referred to in the Article.[5] This is the most blatant form of pay discrimination and may be the most easily identified. It occurs where a male employee and female employee are doing the same or similar work or job but for unequal pay.

---

2. *Defrenne v. Sabena* [1976] E.C.R. 455; *Gerster v. Freistaat Bayern* [1997] I.R.L.R. 699 (ECJ).
3. *Kowalska v. Freie und Hansestadt Hamburg* [1990] I.R.L.R. 447 (ECJ).
4. *Kowalska v. Freie und Hansestadt Hamburg* [1990] I.R.L.R. 447 (ECJ); *Nimz v. Freie Und Hansestadt Hamburg* [1991] I.R.L.R. 222 (ECJ).
5. *Worringham v. Lloyds Bank Limited* [1981] I.R.L.R. 178 (ECJ).

PORTOBELLO COLLEGE LIBRARY
SOUTH RICHMOND STREET
DUBLIN 2.
PHONE 01-4787667

"Work of equal value"

However, the Treaty Article *is not* directly effective where the sex discrimination in pay occurs when the work being done by the man or woman, although different, is nonetheless argued to be of comparative worth. In this case, the discrimination is alleged to be on the basis of unequal pay for work of equal *value*. Although it is covered by Article 141, in this situation, a complaining worker could not simply rely on or plead a breach of Article 141 alone before a national court.

Instead, the secondary rules in the Equal Pay Directive and the implementing national legislation must also be relied on in domestic proceedings to enforce these 'work of equal value' rights before a court in Ireland.[6]

The Directive: Secondary law

A secondary piece of legislation entitled the Equal Pay Directive[7] fleshes out the details of the above Treaty provisions, particularly for the "work of equal value" situation. The Equal Pay Directive contains the legal requirement to have a comparative evaluation system available to employees before national courts. As such, the Directive does not add to the law, but merely facilitates the practical application of the principle in Article 141.[8] This is because where an employee is paid less than an employee of the opposite sex doing a job which, though different, is alleged to be of *comparative worth or value*, the discrimination can

---

6. In Ireland, the implementing national legislation is now the Employment Equality Act 1998. The 1998 Act refers to these distinctions in categories of work under the generic heading of "like work."
7. Directive 75/117 EEC.
8. *Jenkins v. Kingsgate (Clothing Productions) Limited* [1981] I.R.L.R. 228 (ECJ).

only be uncovered by performing an evaluation study that compares the two jobs. However, Article 141 did not contain the details for such a study and was, therefore, held not to be directly effective where the discrimination can only be identified by reference to more explicit implementing provisions.[9] This is precisely what is provided for in the secondary legislation. In particular, the Directive implements the following important rules in relation to the abolition of sex dis-crimination:

- Firstly, Article 1 provides that the principle of equal pay for men and women (for the same work **or** for work to which equal value is attributable) means the elimination of all discrimination on the grounds of sex in regard to all aspects and conditions of remuneration. In particular, where a job classification system is used for determining pay, it must be based on the same criteria for both men and women and so drawn up as to exclude any discrimination on the grounds of sex.

- Secondly, Article 2 provides that Member States shall introduce into their national legal systems such measures as are necessary to enable all employees who consider themselves wronged by a breach of this law to pursue a claim before the courts after possible recourse to other competent authorities.

- Finally, Article 6 requires that the Member States shall take the measures necessary to ensure that the principle of equal pay is applied. They shall see that effective means are available to take care that this principle is observed.

In accordance with Article 6 of the Directive, Irish law has introduced legislation in order to protect employees in

---

9. *Defrenne v. Sabena* [1976] E.C.R. 455.

accordance with the entitlements accorded to them under EU law.

Irish law and the national regime: The practical application of European Law

Employment Equality Act 1998

Irish national law is, in practical terms, the most direct and closest level of protection. Irish law simply domestically incorporates the above requirements of EU law. In particular, Irish law provides, *inter alia*, that a person, irrespective of gender must be paid, at any time, the same rate of remuneration for "**like work.**"[10]

This simply means that, in relation to work which one person is employed to do, another person shall be regarded as employed, whether by the same or an *associated* employer, to do **like work** if:[11]

(a) both perform the same work under the same or similar conditions, or each is interchangeable with the other in relation to work; or

(b) the work performed by one is of a similar nature to that performed by the other and any difference between the work performed or the conditions under which it is

---

10. Section 19(1) of the 1998 Act.
11. The above criteria in section 7(1) of the Employment Equality Act 1998. See also section 7(2) of the 1998 Act whereby it is provided that in relation to the work performed by an agency worker, no person except another agency worker may be regarded as employed to do like work. See section 7(3) where it is provided that, in any case where the remuneration received by one person ("the primary worker") is less than the remuneration received by another ("the comparator"), then, even if the work performed by the primary worker is *greater in value* than the work performed by the comparator, it will simply be treated as if it was *equal in value* anyway.

performed by each either are of small importance in relation to the work as a whole or occur with such irregularity as not to be significant to the work as a whole, or

(c) the work performed by one is equal in value to the work performed by the other, having regard to such matters as skill, physical or mental requirements, responsibility and working conditions.

It is to be noted that the person with whom the discriminated employee is comparing him or herself again must be in the *same or similar position* in terms of the work or job being done by each. In particular, an employee shall not be regarded as doing "like work" with another employee unless they both have the same or reasonably comparable terms and conditions of employment.[12]

Moreover, similarly to EC law, differences in pay can be justified under the 1998 Act where they can be objectively justified by factors unrelated to gender. However, where they cannot be so justified, the pay of the employee in the disadvantaged gender must be *increased* to equalise his or her remuneration with that of the employee whose gender is not so disadvantaged.[13]

The 1998 Act also now requires that it shall be a term of every contract of employment, where A and B are employees, that A shall at any time be entitled to the same rate of remuneration for his work as B, who, at that time or any other relevant time, is employed to do like work as A by the same or an associated employer.[14] As such, this means that, even where a contract does not expressly provide for this or

---

12. See section 19(3) of the 1998 Act. Also see the Labour Court decisions of *Brown v. Eason & Son,* EDA 036 and *Harrington v. East Coast Area Health Board,* EDA 021.

13. Section 19(4) of the 1998 Act.

where an employee does not have a written contract at all, the employee is still entitled to a rate of remuneration that is the same as that of her male comparator.

So, what does "pay" mean? The six basic steps to understanding the rights and duties of "equal pay"

Step One: What is the basic principle?

At first instance, this might appear a very basic question. However, employers and employees should be very careful not to overlook entitlements arising out of the employment relationship that potentially could result in discriminatory treatment in the event that they are not accorded equally to male and female employees. Indeed, there are benefits that fall within the meaning of "pay" that may surprise some employers. This is because, in keeping with the general approach of the European Court of Justice, the meaning of "pay" has been given a very broad meaning.

In short, "pay" comprises any consideration, whether in cash or in kind, whether immediate or future, whether directly or indirectly, that a worker receives in respect of his employment from his employer, whether under a contract of employment, by virtue of legislation or on a voluntary basis.[15]

Step two: To what types of "work" does it apply?

The definition of equal work or work of equal value requires that the person or class of persons seeking equal pay must be able to point to another person or class of persons who,

---

14. Section 20 of the 1998 Act.
15. *Garland v. British Rail Engineering Limited* [1982] I.R.L.R. 111 (ECJ) and *Arbeiterwohlfahrt der Stadt Berlin e.V v. Botel* [1992] E.C.R. I–3589.

although engaged in comparable work, are in a more favourable position in terms of pay. This person or group of persons is known as the "**comparator**."

As such, where might a comparator be found and how do you know what types of work are considered to be the same or of equal value to yours? As such, the general legal framework that answers this question is now outlined below.

The general principles

Firstly, in order to determine whether persons are in fact performing the same or comparable work, it is necessary to take account of the following factors:[16]

- the nature of the activities actually entrusted to each employee;

- the training requirements to carry them out; and

- the working conditions of each employee.

Secondly, although the comparator does not have to be in the same employment or job, he or she must be working in **the same establishment or service**, whether public or private, as the person seeking to rely on him or her in an equal pay claim.[17] In certain circumstances, this criterion may allow for a comparison of the work of two employees but with different employers. As we saw earlier in this chapter, this is reflected in the Employment Equality Act 1998 in Ireland by reference to the criterion that a comparator employee may be employed by the same or *an associated* employer.[18]

Thirdly, the principle that men and women should receive equal pay for equal work is not confined to situations where

---

16. *Brunnhofer v. Bank der Osterrichishen Postparkasse* [2001] I.R.L.R. 571 (ECJ).
17. *Defrenne v. Sabena* [1976] E.C.R. 455 (ECJ).
18. See section 7(1) of the 1998 Act.

the men and women are **contemporaneously** doing equal work or work of equal value for the same employer. Therefore, an employee is permitted to compare him or herself to an employee of the opposite sex who had previously worked for the same employer.[19] As such, an employee in Ireland may include the three years that precede or the three years that follow the time at which he was doing like work as another employee where it is relevant to his claim for equal pay. This entitlement covers not just employees but also persons who are covered by a contract personally to execute any work or labour.[20]

Fourthly, the claim for **equal pay** under EU law traditionally must be based on an **actual** as opposed to a **hypothetical** comparator.[21] However, this principle must be approached cautiously. There are now circumstances which make such a specific comparison unnecessary in every case and, particularly, those concerning the pay of part-time workers. For example, it will be seen that, in a number of cases later in this chapter, that the European Court of Justice did **not** require that a complainant undertake formal proof of a specific comparison between the gender composition of full-time workers as against part-time/job sharer workers in every individual case. The ECJ was willing to simply take judicial notice of the fact *generally* that women are more likely to be engaged in part-time work than men and consequently, any disadvantage imposed on part-time work constitutes, *prima facie*, indirect discrimination. In short, this is a principle that is so well settled, **it does not require full formal proof in court in each specific case**. However, Irish law nonetheless requires that a claim of indirect discrimination in terms of pay must be based *on a comparison* with pay of those of the opposite gender employed, at like work, by

---

19. *McCarthays Limited v. Smith* [1980] E.C.R. 1275 (ECJ).
20. Section 19(2) of the 1998 Act.
21. *McCarthays Limited v. Smith* [1980] E.C.R. 1275 (ECJ).

same or an associated employer. This precise ambiguity, as to the degree to which a comparator is required in a case concerning part-time work, has been specifically noted in a recent Labour Court decision in Ireland.[22]

Fifthly, two groups of employees who have different **professional qualifications** cannot be regarded as employed on the same work for the purpose of Article 141, even where the same activities are performed over a considerable period of time, if the different groups cannot be considered in a comparable situation. Professional training or qualification is not merely one of the factors that may be an objective justification for giving different pay for the same work, it is one of the possible criteria for determining whether the same work is being performed at all.[23]

Finally, the fact that the employees concerned are classified in the same job category under **a collective agreement** is not in itself a sufficient basis for concluding that they perform the same work or work of equal value. The general indications provided in a collective agreement are only one indication amongst others and must, as a matter of evidence, be corroborated by precise and concrete factors based on *the activities actually performed* by the employees concerned.[24]

How these principles are applied in practical terms in Ireland under the Employment Equality Act 1998 may be seen simply in the following case.

---

22. *Eason and Son Limited v. Brown,* ADE 02/1 (No.36). A similar development in Ireland may also be seen in chapter four in relation to equal treatment protection and the absence now of a requirement of formal proof of indirect discrimination for part-time workers and for pregnant employees. See also the Irish Labour Court case of *Inoue v. NBK Designs Limited* [2002] E.L.R. 98.
23. *Angestelltenbetriebsrat v. Wiener Gebeitskrankenkasse* [1999] I.R.L.R. 804 (ECJ).
24. *Brunnhofer v. Bank der Osterrichishen Postparkasse* [2001] I.R.L.R. 571 (ECJ).

Kennedy v. Thurles Golf Club:[25] *Assessing "like pay" under Irish law*

Background This is a case that demonstrates the extent of the detail that will be assessed under Irish law in order to consider whether parties perform "like work." The claimant submitted a claim that she was entitled to the same rate of remuneration as that paid by the respondent to a named male comparator from November 1997 to May 1999 in accordance with section 2 of the Anti-Discrimination (Pay) Act 1974. She claimed that she did like work as did the male comparator prior to his promotion as bar manager. The respondent denied that the claimant was engaged in "like work" with the male comparator, and that there were otherwise grounds other than gender to justify the difference in pay.

Findings The Equality Officer found that the claimant and the comparator were in every way fully interchangeable with each other and, as such, performed like work within the meaning of the 1974 Act.

In doing so, she found, in particular, that the difference in job specifications between them relating to *the ordering of stock* was of small importance in relation to the work as a whole.

She also found that, in this case, *the time* at which the work was carried out did not constitute a ground other than gender. This was because, on the facts here, in paying the claimant and her male comparator, the respondent had not distinguished between *the later and earlier shifts* worked by each of them.

---

25. DEC–E2001–020.

Dublin Institute of Technology v. McEvoy:[26] *Like work:*
The balance of skills and responsibilities

Background The complainant in this case was a employed
as a storekeeper by the respondent. She claimed that she was
entitled to the same rate of remuneration as that paid to a
named male comparator in accordance with section 19 of the
Employment Equality Act 1998, on the basis that she
performed like work as him as defined in section 7(1)(b) and
(c) of the 1998 Act (as set out above). The difference between
the two jobs was that the male comparator technician was
also a trained chef, and it was claimed that he used these
skills and training in the course of his employment in carrying
out his storage and food handling duties. The complainant
was not a trained chef. However, she argued that the cooking
duties undertaken by the comparator were of such an irregular
nature that they were of little importance to the work in
question. Moreover, she pointed out that she also was
responsible for the handling and storage of eggs and dairy
products which involved as much responsibility as that
attributed by the respondent to the comparator.

The respondent denied that the complainant did similar
work as defined in section 7(1)(b) of the 1998 Act or equal
work as defined under section 7(1)(c) of the 1998 Act as the
named male comparator upon which she was relying.

Findings The Labour Court concluded that the comparator
would not have been appointed to the position he held if he
had not been a qualified chef. However, it held that the
important factor in terms of assessing "work of equal value"
was the *actual duties performed* by each party and not their
qualifications.

Therefore, the Labour Court members met with the
comparator and observed the work that he performed. On

26. ADE 0/21, January 21, 2003.

doing so, the court concluded, on the facts, that cooking was a minor *but integral* part of his job overall, and could not be discounted as insignificant. This was not mirrored by any comparable responsibility on the part of the complainant and went beyond what was expected of her.

The court also accepted that the comparator carried greater responsibility in relation to the storage and handling of raw meat, poultry and fish. Although the complainant also handled dairy produce and eggs, the amount of such produce for which she was responsible was small in overall terms. In the case of the comparator, the storage and handling of foodstuffs vulnerable to contamination constituted the bulk of his work.

As such, having balanced these factors, the Labour Court concluded that they were not engaged in like work.

Conclusion As such, the Equality Officer concluded that the respondent had not discriminated against the claimant. This determination, having being appealed to the Labour Court, was upheld.[27]

Step Three: To what extent do the equality rules apply?

No "half-way house" allowed

The application of the principle of equal pay by employers as between men and women in the workplace must be immediate and full. The achievement of equality in relation to pay cannot be made progressive on a basis that still maintains discrimination, even if only temporarily.[28]

In short, if an employee is being discriminated against in terms of his pay, an employer is not permitted to remedy this unlawful treatment by promising to phase in a non-

---

27. See the Labour Court decision of *DIT v. McEvoy*, EDA032, January 21, 2003.
28. *Smith v. Avdel Systems Limited* [1994] I.R.L.R. 602 (ECJ).

discriminatory regime over time. He or she is obliged and must act immediately.

This is an important consideration for all legal practitioners to bear in mind in terms of contesting or settling equal pay claims.

Step four: What types of discrimination are covered?

As outlined briefly earlier, discrimination can take two forms: direct and indirect.

Direct discrimination

This simply means that Article 141 prohibits an employer from paying workers doing the same work, rates of pay that are less favourable according to the sex of the worker. However, it goes further.

Indirect discrimination

It is a general principle of European law that indirect discrimination differs from direct discrimination in that it may be justified by factors unrelated to sex. This is known as "objective justification."

In practice, this means that where the work of two groups can be regarded as simply equal or of equal value, the national court must verify whether there is a substantially higher proportion of one gender than the other in the disadvantaged group. If so, Article 141, the Equal Pay Directive and Irish law require the employer to justify the difference by showing that there are objective reasons for the difference in pay that are unrelated to any discrimination on grounds of sex.[29]

---

29. *Jamstaldhetsombudmannen v. Orebro Lans Landsting* [2000] I.R.L.R. 421(ECJ).

Only arguments that can stand separately from the sex of an employee are relevant.

Hanley and Kelly v. Eircom:[30] *Unequal pay on grounds other than sex: How can you show this?*

Background The Union on behalf of the claimants in this case alleged that they were entitled to the same rate of remuneration as that paid to two male comparators pursuant to section 3 of the Anti-Discrimination (Pay) Act, 1974. This legislation was applied as the grounds of alleged discrimination included periods of time that preceded the introduction of the Employment Equality Act 1998.

The claimants were employed as clerical officers, while the named male comparators were employed as telephone officers. Following restructuring, both these grades had been amalgamated into one grade of Telecom Officer I. The respondent did not contest or concede that the male and female staff did "like work" within the meaning of section 3 of the Act.

However, it did argue that there were grounds other than sex for the difference in pay between the claimants and the male comparator.

Findings The Equality Officer found that the claimants performed "like work" with the two male comparators for the purpose of section 3 of the 1974 Act:

> ***Question One: Is there direct discrimination?***
> In examining the grounds put forward to contend that the different pay was on grounds other than sex under section 2(3) of the 1974 Act, the Equality Officer found that a case of *direct* discrimination had not occurred.

30. DEC–E2001–006 (Equality Tribunal).

Question Two: If not, is there indirect discrimination?

As such, the Equality Officer then addressed the issue of indirect discrimination. She found that, while more females than males had been adversely affected by the payment of a higher rate of pay to former telephone officers, the imbalance was not sufficient to ground a *prima facie* case of *indirect* discrimination.

In reaching this conclusion, the Equality Officer had regard to European law and to a number of leading cases thereunder.

Question Three: What is the difference between "pay" and "treatment."

As a *prima facie* case had not been made out, the Equality Officer held that the respondent was not required to show objectively justifiable grounds for the difference in pay.

The Equality Officer noted other arguments made by the Union in relation to holidays and promotional opportunities, but held that since these issues related to conditions of employment they were instead covered under the "equal treatment" heading (covered at that time specifically under the Employment Equality Act 1977) and not under the Anti-Discrimination (Pay) Act 1974 which related exclusively to pay.

As such, as will be seen below, this is a matter of some complexity and upon which specific legal and other expert advice must be sought. Three sources of indirect discrimination in the workplace are:

a.   the contract of employment.

b.   national legislation.

c.   collective agreements.

Although these three categories comprise the major sources of indirect discrimination to be aware of, it must be borne in mind that the tests, outlined below, applied by the courts to each of them are the same.

The contract of employment

Jenkins v. Kingsgate Limited: *Discrimination: A case of now you see it, now you don't?*[31]

In this seminal case before the European Court of Justice (ECJ), part-time employees received an hourly rate of pay that was lower than that received by full time employees doing the same work. The part-time employees were almost all females. As a result, when looked at directly, the difference was based on the numbers of hours worked, but when looked at indirectly, women were the principal losers.

The ECJ held that, in those circumstances, the choice of such criterion for differential pay rates was capable of violating Article 141. However, it was held that there would be no violation of the principle of equal pay insofar as the difference in pay between part-time work and full-time work is attributable to factors which are objectively justified and are in no way related to any discrimination based on sex.

The ECJ, having outlined the above approach, left the actual decision to the national court in the UK which had referred the question to it. However, it suggested that it might be open to an employer to show that economic reasons encouraged a preference for full time work irrespective of the sex of the worker. In this regard, whereas the intent of an employer is irrelevant in assessing and in defending the *discriminatory effect* of a criterion, an employer is nonetheless entitled to refer to his or her motivation in choosing the criterion in order to demonstrate an *objective justification*.

---

31. [1981] E.C.R. 911 (ECJ).

Bilka-Kaufhaus v. Weber Von Hartz: *Objective justification: Three strikes and you're out?*[32]

This leading case involved an occupational pension scheme operated by the employer privately under the contract of employment, and arose when part-time workers were excluded from its remit unless they could show they had carried out a sufficient amount of full-time work in the past. The employer was a large Department Store. Weber von Hartz, a female employee, did not qualify under this criterion. She argued that women were more likely to work part-time than men due to family responsibilities and that, therefore, the choice of criterion for access to the pension led indirectly to unlawful sex discrimination.

The employer submitted that it was economically justified for it attracted full-time workers rather than part-time workers, by remunerating full-time workers more generously. It was argued in this case that since the part-time workers had a tendency to refuse Saturday work and late afternoons, they were less economically viable.

It was held that national courts must apply **a three-fold test** in assessing the objective justifications submitted by all employers:

1. the measures taken by an employer must correspond to a real and genuine need on the part of the business;

2. the measures are suitable for attaining the objectives of the business;

3. the measures are necessary for that purpose.

If the above three tests are satisfied, then the fact that the measures affect a greater number of members of one gender than another is not enough to amount to a breach of Article 141.

---

32. [1986] E.C.R. 1607.

Moreover, it is vital to bear in mind that this decision sets out the objective justification test as applied generally. As such, this three-fold test is as equally applicable to deciding both equal pay **and** equal treatment cases. Equal treatment will be dealt with at chapters 4 and 5.

Nonetheless, even if one surmounts the above three tests, there are two further stings in the tail for those deemed to have indirectly discriminated against employees on the grounds of sex.

Firstly, the measures adopted must still be *proportionate* to the objective sought. In other words, even if a measure complies with the above three tests, if there is another less discriminatory way to achieve the same objective, the test of proportionately will not be satisfied and the measures will be prohibited.

Secondly, mere *generalisations and assumptions* by employers will not be allowed to justify indirect dis-crimination. An employer has to do more than just make general arguments about the merits of his objectives and the criteria used to implement them, but he just actually prove a direct relationship of cause and effect between his or her objectives and those criteria selected. In *Bilka*, the ECJ specifically rejected the argument of the employer that the exclusion of part-time workers from the pension was necessary, for economic reasons, in order to discourage staff from taking up part-time work. However, it left the final decision itself to the national court in Germany from where the question about the law originally came.

Hill and Stapleton v. The Revenue Commissioners and the Department of Finance:[33] *Differences in pay and the calculation of service: flexible hours, flexible pay?*

Background In this decision of the European Court of

---

33. [1998] E.C.R. I–3739.

Justice relating to the Irish Civil Service,[34] the dispute concerned a rule whereby civil servants who returned to full-time work having completed a period of job-sharing were given a point on the full time pay scale which was lower than that which they had previously occupied when job-sharing.

Findings The European Court of Justice, in finding that there had been discrimination in pay, concisely stated:

> "The regression to which workers are subject when entering or returning to full time work directly affects their pay. ... Consequently, their hourly rate of pay is reduced. Reference to the criterion [relating to hours actually worked during the period of job sharing], as provided for under the scheme applicable here, fails to take account...of the fact that job-sharing is in a unique category as it does not involve a break in service. ... [It also fails to take account] of the fact ... that a job-sharer can acquire the same experience as a full time worker. Furthermore, a disparity is retroactively introduced into the overall pay of employees performing the same functions so far as concerns both the quality and quantity of the work performed. The result of this disparity is that employees working full time but who previously job-shared are treated differently from those who have always worked on a full time basis."

Finally, in terms of the prohibition of less favourable treatment of part-time workers, the position has been greatly enhanced

---

34. This case had come before the ECJ by way of a preliminary reference from the Labour Court under Article 234 of the EC Treaty.

by the enactment of the **Protection of Employees (Part-Time Work) Act 2001** which protects part-time workers in their own right rather than having to rely on a nexus to the gender of the worker. In other words, a worker no longer has to seek protection by bringing herself within the confines only of a sex discrimination claim and the various legal hurdles that involves. As such, part-time working men as well as women now benefit from specific protection of their status.

National legislation

Rinner-Kuhn v. FWW GmbH: *Discrimination and national laws: A veneer of respectability?*[35]

In this case, a provision of German legislation required employers to pay up to six weeks' wages to employees incapable of working due to ill health. However, it allowed for the exclusion of a certain category of employees from this protection. This exclusion was permissible where the employees' contract required no more than 10 hours work weekly or 45 hours work monthly.

Given that more women than men were attracted to employment of this nature, they were disproportionately affected. As such, in keeping with the tests outlined in *Bilka*, it was held that Article 141 precluded national laws from excluding employees in this way when the measure affects a considerably greater number of women than men unless the Member State in question can show that the legislation is justified by objective factors unrelated to sex discrimination. As a result, even though this system of sick pay was a statutory scheme more akin to general social security rather than "pay," the ECJ held that, notwithstanding the statutory background, it was "pay" within the meaning of the Treaty as it was payable by the employer by virtue of the employment relationship.

---

35. [1989] E.C.R. 2743 (ECJ).

Here, the Member State had also argued that workers who worked less than 10 hours per week or 45 hours per month, were not integrated in and connected with the business comparable to that of other workers. This was rejected by the ECJ on the basis that it was only a generalised statement regarding categories of workers, and could not regarded as objective justification unrelated to grounds of sex. It was an inadequate justification and more specific, precise grounds of justification are required.

Collective agreements

Kowalska v. Freie und Hansestadt Hamburg: *The effect of equality: Unravelling the binding agreement*

The principle In this case, it was held that the application of a provision of a collective agreement under which part-time workers were excluded from a benefit, in circumstances where a considerably smaller portion of men than women worked part-time, was prohibited under Article 141 unless the employer had objective justifications unrelated to gender.

It was confirmed that Article 141 is sufficiently precise to be relied upon by an individual employee before a national court in order to have a discriminatory collective agreement set aside. It is for the national court to determine whether and to what extent a provision of an indirectly discriminatory collective agreement is justified on objective grounds unrelated to gender.

No need to renegotiate However, where there is un-justifiable indirect discrimination in a collective agreement, the national court is required to set aside the offending provision, without requesting or awaiting its prior removal by collective negotiation or any other procedure.[36]

---

36. In particular, see *Nimz v. Freie Und Hansestadt Hamburg* [1991] E.C.R. I–297 (ECJ).

It would be incompatible with the nature of Community law for a judge to refuse to do all that was necessary to set aside any provisions of a collective agreement, which might prevent Community standards from attaining their full effect.

Moreover, where there is unjustified indirect discrimination in a provision of a collective agreement, the members of the group that is disadvantaged, must be treated in the same way and have the same system applied to them as to other workers, *in proportion to their hours of work*. This is similarly not a matter for renegotiation but must be ordered directly by the national court.

How this principle applies in practical terms and the meaning of *"in proportion to their hours of pay"* may now be seen from the following two cases.

Eason and Son Limited v. Browne:[37] *Differences in pay: How are they rated?*

Background In this recent Irish Labour Court case, the claimant and her named comparator were employed as sales assistants by the respondent. She was a part-time worker who worked 22.5 hours per week. The comparator was a full-time worker who worked 37.5 hours per week. Under **a collective agreement with SIPTU**, the respondent paid "**service pay**" to employees based on their years of service. Both the claimant and the comparator had more than 20 years service, which was the maximum reckonable for the purpose of the agreement. However, the claimant received a weekly payment in this regard of €2.29 in respect of service. The full time comparator received €3.80 in respect of his service pay. This was 60% of the amount paid to the comparator but was pro-rata to her working hours as against the hours of the full time

---

37. ADE 02/12, March 3, 2003. Labour Court.

comparator. The claimant contended that the service pay was intended to be based on service only and that the practice of the respondent in applying an hours worked qualification, in her case, is discriminatory.

There were a total of 220 sales assistants employed by the respondent, 128 of whom were full-time workers and the remaining 92 were part-time workers. Of the 128 full-time workers 108 were women and 20 were men. All 92 part-time workers were women.

Findings Having assessed the principles from the decisions of the European Court of Justice, the Labour Court was satisfied that, although there were differences in their service pay, the claimant's entitlement to *the same rate of remuneration* as that paid to the comparator was met.

> i. Both were subject to the *same rules* or criteria in the calculation of their overall pay. Entitlement to service pay was determined by the actual number of years worked in both cases. In both cases, while the monetary amount of service pay was expressed as a different weekly rate, that figure could vary downwards depending on the number of hours worked. This applied equally to the claimant and the comparator as well as to full and part-time workers generally;
> ii. Both, in fact, received *the same remuneration* relative to the hours worked.
> iii. The situation would have been different if full time workers were paid a fixed amount that did not vary in relation to the hours worked.

On this basis, the court concluded that the claimant was in receipt of equal pay pursuant to Article 141 and Directive

75/117. This approach is further identified in the following case.

Stadt Lengerich v. Helmig: *Overtime and equal pay: Crossing the collective threshold?*[38]

In this case, however, it was confirmed that it is compatible with Article 141 and with the Equal Pay Directive for a collective agreement to provide for the payment of overtime supplements only for hours worked by *full-time workers* in excess of *their* normal working hours *fixed by agreement*. In other words, this meant that the agreement was justified in excluding any overtime supplements for part-time employees for hours worked *in excess of their individual working hours* but that, nonetheless, did not exceed the number of full-time working hours required in the agreement in order to qualify for overtime supplements.

Look at the bigger picture It was held that such a system was not unequal pay as between part-time and full-time employees since **overall pay was the same for the same number of hours worked** and therefore did not amount to discrimination incompatible with Article 141 or the Directive.

As such, the obligation to provide equal pay can be fulfilled, in the case of part-time workers, by the payment of the same rate as applies to full-time work, adjusted pro-rata to time actually worked. It is important to note that this principle applies generally to the principle of equal pay and is not, of course, limited to only collective agreements.

---

38. [1995] I.R.L.R. 216 (ECJ).

Step five: What types of payment are covered?

Statutory versus occupational benefits

The basic principle Clearly, as Article 141 states, ordinary basic wages and salary are clearly included. However, other supplementary or *ex gratia* perks and benefits of the job are also covered. The absence of any contractual entitlement to such facilities or benefits is irrelevant. Examples of occupational benefits are those provided by employers to employees and relate to sickness, invalidity, old age including early retirement, industrial accidents, occupational diseases and unemployment. Permanent health insurance arrangements, redundancy arrangements and compensation arrangements for work-related illnesses and accidents are all examples of the types of benefits that are covered.

The protection of equal pay between the genders depends not on their legal form, but simply on the fact that they confer a benefit because and arising out of the employment relationship.[39]

The concept of "pay" under Article 141 has a broad definition. In particular, any benefit arising by virtue of the employment relationship is covered.

On the other hand, benefits governed by national laws and financed by the public purse are considered to be social security. Social security is separate to "pay", because it is not then attributable to the employment relationship (no matter how loosely!). Instead, it is deemed to arise from the generally applicable, social policy of the State for all qualifying citizens. It is **statutory**. By way of contrast, the benefits that arise from private contractual employment relationships are considered to be **occupational**. However, things are never that simple!

There is also a third hybrid group where the boundaries are blurred. As we have seen, there are also provisions of

---

39. *Garland v. British Rail Engineering Limited* [1982] E.C.R. 359.

national law that *do* come within the concept of "pay" because
the entitlement to the benefit they create, although having a
statutory basis, has been held to arise from the employment
relationship. Redundancy lump sums are a good example.[40]
As such, they are still considered to be occupational benefits
("pay/occupational social security") rather than statutory
benefits ("state social security").

A very fine line Despite the desire of European Court of
Justice to extend the scope of equality to the greatest extent
possible, it is this obviously fine line of distinction between
the above approaches that has caused many problems in our
understanding of the practical boundaries between the
different types of benefits. This is the case not just for non-
lawyers and but for lawyers also! Indeed, the decision as to
where the line will be drawn can come down to a factual
case-by-case examination.

The solution? Therefore, in order to put some flesh on this
law and bring some certainty to the area, two separate pieces
of secondary legislation were passed to confirm the principle
of equality in terms of state and occupational social security.
The first is called the **State Social Security Directive (79/7)**
and the second is called the **Occupational Social Security
Directive (86/378)**. The first directive applies the principle
of equality to *statutory* benefit payments and schemes. As
will be seen later in this chapter, this directive allowed for a
number of important exemptions from the principle of
equality, particularly, relating to the permissible difference
in retirement ages for state pensions as between men and
women. The second applies the principle of equality to
occupational benefit schemes.[41]

---

40. See *Barber v. Guardian Royal Exchange Assurance Group* [1990]
    I.R.L.R. 240 (ECJ).
41. This has now been amended by Council Directive 96/97EC. It

A guide to the types of payment that cannot, under European Law, be subject to discrimination on the grounds of gender are provided below. However, these are merely examples of a wider spectrum. As such, this is an area upon which specific legal advice should always be sought.

Redundancy lump sums

It has been held that a redundancy payment made by an employer does not cease to constitute a form of pay on the sole ground that, rather than deriving from the contract of employment *per se*, it is a statutory or *ex gratia* payment. Although, these lump sums also reflect the social policy of Member States, as provided in their legislation, they are nonetheless benefits that a worker is entitled to receive from his employer by reason of the existence of the employment relationship.[42] Therefore, all the factors that go to calculating a redundancy lump sum such as the cumulative periods of reckonable service and the rates of the normal weekly wage of an employee must be free of discriminatory distinctions on the grounds of sex unless objectively justified by objective factors unrelated to gender.[43]

Bonuses

A bonus constitutes "pay" within the meaning of Article 141. For example, where the bonus is guaranteed (for example, a Christmas bonus) to employees irrespective of work performance during the year, then it must be paid to all employees even if the contracts of some of those employees

---

was introduced to further clarify the law as will be seen later in this chapter.

42. *Barber v. Guardian Royal Exchange Assurance Group* [1990] I.R.L.R. 240 (ECJ).

43. See the Redundancy Payments Acts 1967–2003.

are in suspension due to their being on parental or maternity leave at the time of payment. Moreover, even where that bonus is awarded retroactively (with past effect) as pay for performance and/or work performed in the course of the year, an employer is precluded from entirely excluding employees either on parental leave or on maternity leave at the time of payment from the benefit of a bonus without taking account of the work already done by them before they went on leave in the year in which the bonus is paid. If bonuses, such as Christmas bonuses, are retroactive pay for work performed, an employer's refusal to award this bonus to workers on maternity/parental leave, who worked during the year in which the bonus was granted, on the sole basis that their contract of employment was suspended when the bonus was granted, constitutes discrimination within the meaning of Article 141, since female workers are far more likely to be on parental leave (and, by definition, on maternity leave) when the bonus is awarded than male workers. It places them at a disadvantage as compared with those whose contract is not suspended at the time of the award.[44]

Job classifications

A system for classifying workers on their return from job-sharing/part-time to full-time employment, that results in the position of those workers being lowered on the incremental pay scale, can come indirectly within the concept of "pay" in Article 141 since the classification determines the progression of pay.[45]

---

44. *Lewen v. Denda* [2000] I.R.L.R. 67 (ECJ).
45. *Hill and Stapleton v. The Revenue Commissioners* [1998] E.L.R. 225.

Sick pay

General illness As seen earlier, while there is still no automatic general entitlement to sick pay, the continued payment of wages to a worker in the event of illness under a contractual scheme falls within the definition of pay within the meaning of Article 141. As such, the rules of the sick pay scheme cannot discriminate on the grounds of gender unless such discrimination can be objectively justified by factors unrelated to sex.

Pregnancy-related illness It is contrary to Article 141 and the Equal Pay Directive to deprive a woman of her full pay, when she is unfit for work prior to the commencement of her maternity leave due to a pregnancy related illness when other employees in the workplace are, in principle, entitled to receive full pay in the event of incapacity for work on grounds of illness.

Travel concessions

Facilities, such as travel concessions accorded to employees are "pay" within the meaning of Article 141. Therefore, an employer, who provided special travel facilities to former male employees to enjoy after their retirement, discriminated against former female employees who did not receive the same facilities.

Notice entitlements

Sums payable by an employer to an employee for failing to give notice to which an employee is entitled are covered, because such payments are in respect of an employee's employment.[46] The calculation of notice entitlements cannot

---

46. *Clark v. Secretary of State For Employment* [1995] I.R.L.R. 421 (English EAT decision).

discriminate on the grounds of gender unless objectively justified by factors unrelated to sex.

Unfair dismissal compensation

An **award** of unfair dismissal compensation constitutes "pay" within the meaning of Article 141 since it is paid to an employee by reason of employment that would have continued but for the unfair dismissal. Moreover, the **conditions** that determine whether an unfairly dismissed employee is entitled to compensation are covered by the equal pay rules.[47] For example, an employer cannot rely on prior discrimination in pay as between men and women doing equal work or work of equal value in calculating the financial loss of an unfairly dismissed male or female employee or by seeking to limit any finding of financial loss by a Tribunal to the lower discriminatory rate of pay. Therefore, it is always advisable, especially where the tenure of a dismissed employee is part-time or on job share, to seek information on the rates of pay from the employer prior to the hearing of a claim in order to confirm that discriminatory rates of pay are not being relied upon. This is all the more so where the employer is in the private sector.

Paid leave and overtime pay

Compensation in the form of paid leave or overtime pay for participation in training courses given by employers to staff committee members can fall within the meaning of Article 141 and the Equal Pay Directive, even where such payments are made in accordance with statutory provisions. This is because, although such compensation does not arise from the contract of employment, it is nonetheless paid by the

47. *R v. Secretary of State for Employment, ex parte Seymour-Smith* [1999] I.R.L.R. 253 (ECJ).

employer by virtue of legislative provisions and by reason of the existence of the employment relationship between the parties.[48]

Maternity leave pay

The benefit paid by an employer to a woman on maternity leave constitutes "pay" within the meaning of Article 141 and the Equal Treatment Directive. Moreover, a woman on maternity leave, when returning, **must** also receive any pay rise awarded before or during her maternity leave. However, the principle of equal pay does not require that a woman should continue to receive her full pay during maternity leave. It is for national legislation to set the amount of maternity pay, provided the amount is not so low as to undermine the purpose of maternity leave, namely the protection of women before and after giving birth. In order to assess the adequacy of the amount payable, the national court must take into account other forms of social protection afforded by national law in the case of justified absence from work as well as the length of maternity leave.[49]

Step six: What other benefits fall within your "pay"?

As well as the above types of payment, identifying whether other types of benefit fall within the definition of "pay" is an issue that has caused much debate and even greater legal confusion over the years in Europe.

---

48. *Arbeiterwohlfahrt der Stadt Berlin e.V v. Botel* [1992] E.C.R. I–3589.
49. *Gillespie v. Northern Health and Social Services Board* [1996] I.R.L.R. 214 (ECJ).

Pensions versus pay

However, the benefit that has caused the most difficulties in classifying is the humble pension. On the one hand, the basic principle is that pensions constitute "pay" where they are purely private in nature. In other words, when its terms and conditions are entirely covered by the contract of employment. On the other hand, Article 141 does not control benefits governed directly by legislation, that are compulsory for general categories of workers in society and that operate with no element of internal agreement within the business or the trade. As such, a retirement or old-age pension established entirely under a state social security scheme created by legislation falls outside the concept of "pay."[50] However, like other hybrid occupational benefits outlined above, the problem is that many private pension schemes operate in addition to the State pension scheme, have at least some state support and in many cases are actually organised by the State.

Why is this distinction so important, anyway?

If a pension falls outside the scope of "pay" within the meaning of Article 141, it is considered to be social security and subject to a derogation from the principle of equality. This derogation, expressly provided for in the Social Security Directive (Directive 79/7), allows for inequality in relation to the determination of pensionable ages between men and women for the purposes of granting old age and retirement pensions. However, if a pension is considered to be pay no such difference in treatment is permitted.

Moreover, the factors relied on by the ECJ in answering the pensions question and in setting the boundaries as to what is "pay" and what is 'social security" are most important to

---

50. *Defrenne v. Belgium* [1971] E.C.R. 445 (ECJ).

our understanding of what constitutes "pay" generally and are now set out below:

Bilka-Kaufhaus v. Weber von Hartz. The supplemental pension scheme: Publicly Inspired, privately agreed[51]

The facts In this case, the employer had established its own retirement pension scheme for its employees.

a. The Scheme had been set up voluntarily as a result of an agreement reached internally within the business.

b. Entitlements were payable under the contract of employment.

c. The Scheme *supplemented* the benefits payable to employees under generally applicable national legislation with benefits that were *financed entirely by the employer*.

Conclusion The ECJ concluded that this was "pay" and subject to the requirement of equality between the sexes. As such, discrimination against part-time workers in accessing this Scheme would have to be justified in accordance with the Treaty. In this regard, the Court, however, warned that this rule does not have the effect of requiring an employer to organise an occupational pension scheme in such a manner as to take into account the particular difficulties faced by persons with family responsibilities in meeting the conditions for entitlement to such a pension. This was because Article 141 and the Directive are restricted simply to the issue of "pay" only and not to other surrounding factors relating to equal treatment.

This decision held that Article 141 applied to private pensions that simply supplemented State pensions.

---

51. [1986] E.C.R. 1607.

But what about pensions schemes that not only supplemented, but entirely replaced the State pension?

This is known as "contracting out." It simply means that parties can exercise a statutory option to replace the State pension, to which they already had a legal entitlement, with a pension paid by the employer in substitution for and improvement on, the State pension. In the era of privatisation, this question could no longer be ignored.

Barber v. Guardian Royal Exchange: Contracting out of social security: The privatisation of inequality?

In this seminal decision, the pension plan in question had been "contracted out" of a State scheme. Whereas the law generally required that a pension be paid to employees like Mr Barber, the parties had decided to take the matter into the private sphere of the contractual relationship.

Mr Barber was a member of the contracted out pension scheme established by his employer. In the category of employees to which he belonged, there was a differential retirement age for men and for women. Mr Barber was made redundant at the age of 52 years. He received a statutory redundancy benefit and cash benefits as well as benefiting from a *deferred* pension. However, under the terms of the scheme, a woman of his age and in the same circumstances would have received an *immediate* pension as well as the statutory redundancy and the cash benefits. Mr Barber argued that this differential treatment was unjustifiable discrimination on the grounds of sex. However, the problem was that UK did allow for a difference in treatment in retirement ages for men and women so long as contracted out pensions could be considered as social security. This United Kingdom position appeared to have been endorsed in EC legislation itself.[52]

---

52. See, EC Directive 79/7 on the Progressive Implementation of the Principle of Equal Treatment for Men and Women in Matters of

Therefore, the issue came down to the following question:

Can an occupational pension scheme contracting out of a state scheme get around Article 141 by importing State protected inequality into the private employment relationship of workers?
Despite Directive 79/7 on Social Security, the ECJ firmly held that it could not. It was held that occupational pension schemes of this nature would from now on constitute "pay" since it was held that, although they replaced a public scheme, they were nonetheless received by reason of the employment relationship. As such, they were occupational schemes covered by the rules on gender equality.[53]

Conclusion This meant that Mr Barber, who, by virtue of the difference in statutory retirement ages, had been denied a pension where a female employee would have received one, was a victim of discrimination on the grounds of his gender.

Fall out However, given this major change in the law, it was clear to the Court that its unlimited application would have caused undue confusion and financial disruption. As such, the ECJ limited its application by providing that Article 141 could not be relied on in order to claim an equal entitlement to benefits under a pension for periods of service prior to the date of this judgment, except where the proceedings had already issued. In order to clarify what this meant a Protocol to the Maastricht Treaty now states that benefits under occupational pension schemes shall not be

---

Social Security and Directive 86/378 on Equal Treatment for Men and Women in Occupational Social Security Schemes.
53. See now the new Council Directive 96/97/EC Amending Directive 86/378/EEC. This new Directive implements the judgment in *Barber* and covers benefits intended to supplement or replace benefits provided by statutory social security schemes.

considered as remuneration if and insofar as they are attributable to periods of employment prior to May 17, 1990. This simply means that the direct effect of Article 141, as discussed above, may now only be used, for the purposes of claiming equal pay in relation to occupational pensions, in respect of pension benefits payable for periods of service in employment *from May 17, 1990 onwards* unless an employee had already started his or her own case before that date.[54]

A short summary of the new rules

It is not within the remit of this book to provide an in-depth analysis of all pension rights currently in force in Ireland.[55] However, in relation to equal pay, the following is a summary of the current law:

a. *What is the effect of this May 17, 1990 Protocol?*

In short, this Protocol says that you are not entitled to rely on the principle of equal pay to be applied to benefits under occupational schemes arising from your period of employment before May 17, 1990 unless you had legal proceedings in being before that day (May 17, 1990) seeking equal pay in the provision of those benefits.

However, three important instances when discrimination is still impermissible before May 17, 1990 in relation to occupational pension schemes, are:

i. When the discrimination relates not to the *benefits* payable under the pension scheme

---

54. *Ten Oever v. Stichting Bedrijfspensioenfonds* [1993] I.R.L.R. 601 (ECJ).

55. In Ireland, the primary law in this area is found in the Pensions Act 1990.

**as assessed in *Barber* but simply to the right
of *access* to that scheme as assessed in *Bilka*.**

Barber versus *Bilka*?

Article 141 covers both the right to join a pension scheme as
well as the benefits payable under them. Since neither the
Protocol in the Maastricht Treaty providing for the above
cut-off date nor the *Barber* decision deal with the issue of
membership for occupational schemes, this access entitlement
continues to be dealt with under the *Bilka* decision to which
the arbitrary May 17, 1990 date does **not** apply. This means
that if the specific infringement of the principle of equal pay
relates to the unlawful exclusion of an employee from an
occupational pension scheme, the employee remains entitled
to retrospective membership of the pension scheme as if he
were never excluded. This has two mixed implications for
employees. On the one hand, this is favourable to such
employees as the time limitation on this type of claim of
membership discrimination is **April 8, 1976**[56]. In other words,
you can go as far back as this date in order to show that you
were discriminated against in getting access to a scheme. On
the other hand, it creates a disadvantage. This is because even
though an employee can claim membership of an occupational
pension scheme retrospectively, it does not mean that he or
she avoids paying all the contributions for the period of
membership of which he was deprived. He or she will have
to do this in order to get the same benefits as those who were
not excluded. The employee cannot claim more favourable
treatment, particularly in financial terms, than if he or she

---

56. This is the date of the decision in *Defrenne (No. 2)* [1976] E.C.R.
455 that establishes this right. In *Schroder v. Deutshe Telecom AG*
[2000] I.R.L.R. 353 (ECJ), the Court confirmed this as the legal
position.

had been duly accepted as a member.[57] It is the disadvantaged employee who must "catch up" in his contributions if he wishes to avail of the same pension entitlements!

ii. **When a benefit is not linked to the actual length of service. In a case such as a lump sum payment in the event of an employee's death during employment, the limitation in *Barber* applies only where the operative event (i.e. the death) occurred before May 17, 1990.** After that date, such benefits must be granted in accordance with the principle of equal pay without distinguishing between periods of service prior to and subsequent to the *Barber* judgment since the length or date of service is not relevant to the calculation of the lump sum.[58]

iii. **When other forms of discrimination, that could never have been considered as permissible under EC law, are at issue.** The time limitation in the *Barber* judgment concerns only discrimination that employers and trustees *could reasonably have considered to be permissible* as a result of the exception allowed under Community law for the determination of the different pensionable ages for men and women.[59] For example, it has been

---

57. For the most important caselaw in this area, read in more detail: *Vroege v. NCIV* [1994] I.R.L.R. 651 (ECJ); *Fisscher v. Voorhuis Hengelo BV* [1994] I.R.L.R. 662 (ECJ); *Dietz v. Stichting Thuiszorg Rotterdam* [1996] I.R.L.R. 692 (ECJ); *Schroder v. Deutshe Telecom AG* [2000] I.R.L.R. 353 (ECJ).

58. *Coloroll Pension Trustees Limited v. Russell* [1994] I.R.L.R. 586 (ECJ).

59. It may be recalled from earlier in this section that the Social

clear since the judgment in *Bilka* that any
discrimination, based on sex, relating to the
right of an employee *to join* a pension scheme
infringes Article 141. As such, there was *never
any reason for employers* to have been
mistaken about the prohibition of this type of
discrimination, and, where it is challenged, as
we saw at (i) above, the claim will not be
limited only to dates after May 17, 1990.
However, once again, it is up to the employee
to catch up on his contributions in order to
secure the same benefits he would otherwise
have been entitled to, had he not been excluded.

b. *Is levelling up the only answer? Eradicating the inequalities in the scheme*

Article 141 does not preclude measures that achieve equal
treatment by reducing the advantages of the person previously
favoured. It merely requires that men and women receive the
same pay for the same work without imposing any specific
level of pay. For example, Article 141 does not preclude an
employer from raising the retirement age for men and women
in order to comply with the *Barber* judgment. However, when
equality is achieved in this way, Article 141 does not allow
for interim or transitional measures designed to ease or limit
the adverse consequences for women (or men, depending on
the situation) as regards their benefits in respect of periods
of service into the future.[60]

Once discrimination in pay has been found to exist, so
long as the measures for bringing about equal pay are not

Security Directive 79/7 allowed countries to set different
pensionable ages for men and women in relation to contracted out
pension schemes. After *Barber*, this was impermissible.
60. *Smith v. Avdel Systems Limited* [1994] I.R.L.R. 602 (ECJ).

adopted in the Scheme, the only way of complying with Article 141 is to grant the employees in the disadvantaged class the same advantages as those enjoyed by the employees in the favoured class. Therefore, this means, for example, that during the period between the *Barber* decision and the date on which a scheme finally adopted measures to achieve equality in relation to the pensionable age, the pension rights of the disadvantaged gender must be calculated on the same basis as those of the favoured gender. In particular, an employer or trustee cannot get around the extra financial burden in this way by deeming such equality measures, when finally implemented, as also retroactive to any interim period before they were so implemented.[61]

c. *Are civil service pension schemes covered by equality rules?*

Given that the law places much emphasis on the private nature of occupational pensions in defining them as "pay," it might have been thought that civil service/public authority pensions would fall outside the protection of the law on equal pay. However, a civil service pension scheme also forms part of the pay of an employee and comes within Article 141. This is the case even though such pensions are governed entirely by public law. If the pension paid by the public employer concerns a particular category of workers only, if it is directly related to the period of service and if its amount is calculated by reference to a public servant's last salary, it is entirely comparable to the pension paid by a private employee to his or her employees. As such, Article 141 precludes national legislation from applying different rules to the calculation of an occupational pension for married men and women. Married men placed at a disadvantage by this discrimination are

---

61. *Smith v. Avdel Systems Limited* [1994] I.R.L.R. 602 (ECJ).

entitled to be treated in the same way and have the same scheme applied to them as married women.[62]

d. *What are the duties of trustees of an occupational pension scheme?*

Article 141 may be relied upon against the trustees of an occupational pension scheme. Since such trustees are required to provide benefits which are "pay" within the meaning of Article 141, they are bound, in doing so, to carry out everything within the scope of their powers to ensure compliance with the principle of equal pay. As such, employers and trustees cannot rely on the rules of their pension scheme or the deed of trust in order to evade their obligations at law in the matter of pay.

Insofar as any of our national laws in Ireland prohibit trustees from acting beyond the scope of their powers or in disregard of the provisions of the trust deed, employers and trustees are bound to use all the means available under domestic law to ensure compliance with the principle of equal pay, such as recourse to the national courts to amend the provisions of the pension scheme or of the trust deed.[63]

e. *Don't women live longer than men? Taking account of actuarial statistics*

Earlier, in the discussion about indirect sex discrimination, it may be recalled that the ECJ held that it was not possible to justify such discrimination by reference to generalisations and assumptions. It required specific, precise justification before indirect discrimination was permissible in a particular case. However, in an example of its sometimes contradictory

---

62. *Bestuur van het Algemeen v. Beaune* [1995] I.R.L.R. 103 (ECJ).
63. *Coloroll Pension Trustees Limited v. Russell* [1994] I.R.L.R. 586 (ECJ).

jurisprudence, the ECJ, in the context of pension entitlements, does indeed allow differences in treatment to be justified by reference to generalised actuarial statistics unrelated to the particular circumstances of the claimants before it.

This is a matter of some considerable complexity and outside the remit of this book. It is a matter upon which specific legal and actuarial advice should always be sought. Nonetheless, the fact that this area of law is still in considerable development is beyond doubt.

FUTURE EQUAL PAY AND PENSION DEVELOPMENTS

Given the complexity and extent to which the ECJ considered the issue of pension entitlements and their relationship to "pay," it is little wonder that this area of law has now once again given rise to one of the most important and potentially controversial cases in recent times. Indeed, the following case has significant repercussions far beyond the more limited field of equal pay cases and now, as always, overrides all countervailing national law.

K.B. v National Health Service Pensions Agency and the Secretary of State for Health.[64] Rolling out the boundaries of equal pay: Sex discrimination and the institution of marriage

Background

This was a case that came before the ECJ by way of a reference under Article 234 of the EC Treaty from the Court of Appeal of England and Wales for a preliminary ruling in proceedings before that court.

---

64. Judgment of the European Court of Justice, C–117/01, January 7, 2004.

KB, the claimant in the main proceedings in England, was a woman who had worked for approximately 20 years for the NHS, *inter alia*, as a nurse and was a member of the NHS pension scheme. KB had shared an emotional and domestic relationship for a number of years with R, a person born a woman and registered as such in the Register of Births. Following surgical gender reassignment, R had become a man. However, R had not been allowed under English law to amend his birth certificate to reflect this change officially. As a result, and, contrary to their wishes, both KB and R were unable to get married. KB gave evidence that their relationship was celebrated in an adapted ceremony approved by a bishop of the Church of England and both KB and R exchanged vows of a type that would be used by any other couple entering into marriage.

However, the problem of the legal status of their long-term relationship remained. In particular, the NHS Pension Scheme Regulation 1995 provided that if a female member of the Scheme died in certain circumstances and left a surviving widower, the widower was, in principle, entitled to a survivor's pension. Although, under the Scheme, "widower" was not defined, it was not disputed that, under English law, the term referred to a person *married* to the Scheme member. As such, on enquiry by KB about her situation, she was informed by the NHS Pensions Agency that, as she and R were not married, if she were to predecease him, R would not be able to receive his widower's pension since it was only payable to a spouse and there was no provision under English law to recognize someone as a "spouse" in the absence of a lawful marriage.

KB took proceedings, invoking Article 141 and Directive 75/117, against this policy. They ultimately ended up before the Court of Appeal. She contended, *inter alia*, that these national provisions of English law restricting survivors' pension rights to only widowers and widows of Scheme members (in other words, surviving spouses) amounted to

discrimination based on sex. The Court of Appeal stayed
proceedings until it got an answer from the ECJ on the
following question:

> "Does the exclusion of the female-to-male
> transsexual partner of a female member of the
> National Health Service Pension Scheme, which
> limits the material dependant's benefit to her
> widower, constitute sex discrimination in
> contravention of Article 141 and Directive 75/
> 117?"

Findings

The ECJ held the Pension Scheme unlawful. In doing so, it
rejected the primary arguments of the UK Government and
even of the European Commission that KB was not entitled
to the benefit of protection under Article 141 and Directive
75/117. Moreover the Commission had argued that this case
involved the definition of "marriage" under family law and
as such remained within the competence of the Member States
only.

In this regard, the Court was careful to say that national
policies that restrict certain benefits to married couples only
was not unlawful and that this was a matter for the national
legislature and courts. Here, however, it distinguished that
situation from the one in this case.

**In short, it essentially held that, if the Member States
want to make marriage a criterion for the restriction of
certain benefits that can also amount to "pay" under EC
law, then they cannot also now restrict, under their legal
arrangements, the right of access (for transsexuals at
least) to getting married.**

In other words, the ECJ held that, although this case did
not directly undermine enjoyment of a right protected under
Community law, it affected the conditions for the grant of

that right. The inequality did not relate to the award of the widower's pension *per se* but to a necessary precondition for the grant of such a right, namely, the capacity to marry.

In this regard, the ECJ stated that a heterosexual couple, where neither partner's identity is the result of gender reassignment surgery, is able to marry and, as the case may be, have the benefit of survivor's pension which forms part of the pay of one of them. However, KB and R were unable to satisfy the marriage requirement, as laid down by the NHS Pension Scheme, for the purpose of the award of the survivor's pension. In this regard, they also stated that the fact that the pension, by definition, is not paid to the employee but to the employee's survivor does not affect the interpretation of "pay" because such a benefit, being an advantage deriving from the fact that the spouse of the survivor was a member of the scheme, meant that the pension is vested in the survivor by reason of the employment relationship and is paid to the survivor by reason of the employment of the spouse.

With very fundamental consequences, the ECJ then held that the fact that it was impossible for KB and R to marry was due to the following:

i. The Matrimonial Causes Act 1973 in England which deems a marriage void if the parties are not respectively male and female;

ii. At law, R's sex was deemed to be that appearing on his birth certificate;

iii. This was because the Births, Deaths and Registration Act did not allow for any alteration of the register of births except in the case of a clerical error or an error of fact.

In these circumstances, the ECJ had regard to the fact that the European Court of Human Rights (ECHR) had already found this situation in England (and, indirectly in Ireland) to be a breach of Article 12 of the European Convention on Human Rights on the right to marry. It then concluded that the above legislation which, in breach of the ECHR, prevented a couple, such as KB and R, who were, at law, still a same sex couple, from fulfilling the marriage requirement must also be regarded, in principle, as being incompatible with the overriding requirements of Article 141.

In doing so, the ECJ conclusively held that Article 141, in principle, now precludes legislation of the type at issue here, which in breach of the European Convention on Human Rights, prevents a couple such as KB and R from fulfilling the marriage requirement, which must be met for one of them to be able to benefit from part of the pay of the other.

The matter was then remitted back to the Court of Appeal in London to decide if KB and R fell within the protection of this new principle.

Lessons?

As will be appreciated, this decision has implications far beyond the realm of equal pay in terms of our taxation, administration and constitutional regime in Ireland. Nonetheless, even within the terms of equal pay, it has very serious consequences for how pension schemes and other work related benefits are operated. There are a number of clear lessons from this case:

> i. There is nothing unlawful about making marriage the criterion for access to benefits or to the payment thereof under a particular scheme of work-related remuneration;
>
> ii. However, if marriage is the criterion, access to the institution of marriage, in turn, cannot now be restricted (in the case of transsexuals at least).

iii. The Member States can decide, if they so wish, to refrain from using marriage criteria in order to regulate right of access to remuneration benefits. However, if they do so, they must use alternative criteria that are not related to gender, either directly or indirectly.

iv. It remains to be seen what effect this case will have on the issue of recognizing same sex unions generally (as distinct from the narrower issue of transgender realignment as here). There are a number of ways that Member States can rectify this situation without legally recognizing same sex unions *per se*. The most obvious one is to now allow transsexuals to change their gender legally in England and Ireland thereby recognizing couples like KB and R as being in a heterosexual, rather than homosexual, relationship. However, it is not clear from this decision if this is now going to be enough for the ECJ. Certainly, in a previous case, it held that gay and lesbian couples generally were not within the remit of those recognized for protection under Article 141 (simply because of a narrower definition of what that Article meant by "gender" discrimination).[65] However, this decision is now six years old and it is clear that the ECJ has moved significantly closer to such recognition in this case.

v. As such, this case and Article 141 are now guaranteed to be the source of future legal

---

65. See the case of *Grant* [1998] E.C.R. I–621.

developments (and probably heated discussion) over the coming years.

Therefore, having discussed the fundamental principle of
equal pay, its development both under European law and Irish
law and its current scope, we now turn in the next chapter to
the second pillar of the protection against sex discrimination
in the workplace, equal treatment.

CHAPTER 4

Equality of Treatment: The Building Blocks Of Our Common Identity?

This area is different to that of equal pay in that it covers all other types of treatment which, although not related to pay directly, nonetheless affect the terms and conditions of employment of an employee.

Once again, the primary law applicable in this area is European law which, in turn, is incorporated through domestic legislation into Ireland.

EUROPEAN LAW: THE EQUAL TREATMENT DIRECTIVE 76/207

Article 2(1) of the Equal Treatment Directive provides that:

> "there shall be no discrimination whatsoever on grounds of sex, either directly or indirectly by reference in particular to family or marital status."

This principle applies to access to employment, including promotion, vocational training and working conditions. It also applies to all types of employment, including employment in the public service.

It is also clear that it applies, like the principle of equal pay, to both direct and indirect discrimination. As such, these two terms bear the same meaning in the context of equal treatment as they do in the context of equal pay. Moreover, as with equal pay, a **comparator** is normally necessary in order to found a complaint of unequal treatment. The same principles relating to comparators as discussed in chapter three on equal pay would similarly apply here.

In particular, there also appear to be circumstances here so settled at law or that effect women to such a degree that a court does not (or even ought not) require a **specific** male comparator or specific, detailed statistical evidence for each case before making a finding of sex discrimination. In other words, courts do not require full formal proof. This is as much to do with avoiding injustice to parties bringing sex discrimination cases as it is with formulating settled legal principles. However, the obvious question that may be asked is how this approach itself complies with the *prima facie* burden of proof requirements on all complainants in each case of this nature and as discussed in chapter two. This is a valid question and one with which the courts themselves have struggled. This may be seen from the following cases.

Although this case was decided before the introduction of the Burden of Proof Directive 97/80, in *Perera v. Civil Service Commission*,[1] Mr Justice Browne-Wilkinson determined, in relation to a case dealing with indirect discrimination before the English Employment Appeals Tribunal and where sufficient statistical evidence had not been adduced, the following:

> " … [T]here remains the root problem that, by any normal statistical standards, the only statistical evidence laid before the [EAT] is in fact inadequate. It is based on a very small sample from a very small number of non-typical offices. Is it therefore right to hold that the complainant

---

1. [1982] I.R.L.R. 147.

has proved her case? We have this very difficult point. On the one hand, the burden is on the complainant to prove his case and, viewed in isolation, the statistics produced do not prove it. On the other hand, it is most undesirable that, in all cases of indirect discrimination, elaborate statistical evidence should be required before the case can be found proved. The time and expense involved in preparing and proving statistical evidence can be enormous, as experience in the United States has demonstrated ...".

A similar approach may be discerned from the following ECJ decision.

Dekker v. VJV-Centrum Plus:[2] **Pregnancy: A stand alone condition**

Background In this case, a woman was refused a job on the grounds that she was pregnant. However, the successful candidate was another woman and there were no male candidates at all in the interview process who had applied for the position.

Findings The ECJ nonetheless found that sex discrimination had occurred in this case. It determined that since only a woman can ever be refused employment because of her pregnancy (irrespective of the comparator), such a refusal constituted discrimination on the grounds of sex.

From this approach, it appears that the position of a *pregnant* woman cannot be compared at law with that of a man similarly medically incapable.[3]

---

2. [1990] E.C.R. I–3491.

3. *Webb v. Belgium* [1994] E.C.R. 3567.

As such, the manner in which the Irish courts and tribunals have dealt with this complex question of discrimination and statistical/comparator evidence in equal treatment cases under the Employment Equality Act 1998 is discussed in more detail below.

Moreover, as well as the above general principles relating to equal treatment, the following specifically are also covered.

Access to employment and vocational training

Articles 3 and 4 of the Directive provide, *inter alia*, that the principle of equal treatment under the Directive applies to conditions of access to employment, including the selection criteria, to all jobs or posts, whatever the sector or branch of activity and to all levels of the occupational hierarchy. The principle of equal treatment also applies to all levels of vocational training, guidance and retraining.

Working conditions

Article 5 of the Directive applies to *working conditions*, including those conditions that govern promotion. It also includes dismissal situations. It has been held that a dismissal in this context should be widely construed so as to include *any* termination of the employment situation, even as part of a voluntary redundancy scheme.[4]

Compulsory retirement also falls within the scope of Article 5. As such, it has been held unlawful for an employer to have different retirement ages for his male and female workforce.[5]

---

4. *Burton v. British Railways* [1982] E.C.R. 555.
5. *Marsall v. Southampton Area Health Authority* [1986] E.C.R. 273.

Derogations

There are three exceptions to the equal treatment principle permitted by the Directive.

Nature of the job test

Firstly, where, by reason of the nature of the job or the context in which it is performed, the sex of the worker constitutes a determining factor.[6]

Maternity and pregnancy rights

Secondly, where women need to be protected particularly as regards pregnancy and maternity.[7] This might seem to be an almost self-explanatory protection and is necessarily an extension of the protection of the safety, health and welfare of female employees at work.[8] However, it has led to some complex issues such as, for example, the availability or otherwise of the rights under this heading to, for example, a male partner of a female employee and the relationship between pregnancy and maternity related absences from work and absences generally by reason of ill health. In other words, does there come a point in law when pregnancy and maternity can no longer justify the absence from work of female employees, *even if* the illness is actually pregnancy or maternity related? The answer is yes. Moreover, is it always

---

6. Article 2(2) of the Directive. See the leading ECJ case of *Johnston v. RUC* [1986] E.C.R. 1651. This derogation is also provided for under Irish law by section 25 of the Employment Equality Act 1998.

7. Article 2(3). This derogation is also available under Irish law in section 26 of the Employment Equality Act 1998.

8. See, in particular, the Irish Maternity Protection (Time Off for Ante- and Post-Natal Care) Regulations 1995 (S.I. No.18 of 1995) and the Safety, Health and Welfare at Work (Pregnant Employees) Regulations 2000 (S.I. No.218 of 2000).

unlawful to dismiss a female employee on grounds of incapacity for work when the reason for the absence is a pregnancy related illness? While employers should exercise extreme caution, the answer is no. As such, the following cases illustrate the scope and purpose of this exemption.

The right of paternity?

Hofman v. Barmer Ersatzkasse.[9] Paternity leave and the special maternal relationship

Background In this leading case of the European Court of Justice ("ECJ"), the claimant father had taken paternity leave to look after his newborn child while the mother, having completed the full, obligatory period of maternity leave, decided to return to work. When the father claimed the statutory "maternity" allowance, which was otherwise payable to mothers in the same circumstances, he was refused. He instituted proceedings claiming unequal treatment contrary to the Directive and EC Treaty.

Findings The ECJ confirmed that Article 2(3) permitted Member States to introduce provisions designed to protect:

> "... [both] a woman's biological condition during pregnancy and thereafter until such time as her physiological and mental functions have returned to normal after childbirth ... [and] to protect the special relationship between a woman and her child over the period which follows between pregnancy and childbirth, by preventing the relationship being disturbed by the multiple burdens which would result from the simultaneous pursuit of employment."

---

9. [1984] E.C.R. 3047.

As a result, the ECJ held that the Equal Treatment Directive did not require a Member State to grant paternity leave to fathers, *even where* the parents so decide. In doing so, the ECJ further confirmed that the Member States had a discretion within the framework laid down by the Directive, to protect women in connection with pregnancy and maternity and to offset the disadvantage which women, in comparison to men, suffer with regard to the retention of employment.

This position is incorporated into Irish law pursuant to the terms of the **Maternity Protection Act 1994**, in terms of the entitlement of a pregnant employee to take 18 weeks leave and thereafter her entitlement to return to the same job or to suitable alternative employment as she was doing immediately prior to her taking leave. This Act also allows for differences in treatment for women in the workplace arising before maternity leave and is motivated by health and safety considerations.

Moreover, the position in relation to paternity leave and the differences in treatment between men and women has softened somewhat since the passing into law in Ireland of the **Parental Leave Act 1998**, which is gender-neutral in relation to the entitlement, subject to a number of conditions, to take leave to care for a young child. However, this leave remains unpaid.[10]

Scope of maternity protection rights

However, even in relation to the maternity and pregnancy rights accorded to women, although very strict, they are not, by any means, open-ended.

The settled principle in relation to this area was set out very clearly in *Brown v. Rentokil*.[11] In this case, dealing with

---

10. See also, the Adoptive Leave Act 1995 and the Carers' Leave Act 2001.
11. [1998] E.C.R. I–4185.

the point at which an employer is entitled to treat pregnancy related ill health in the same way as "ordinary" illness generally for the purposes of effecting a fair dismissal on the grounds of incapacity for work, the European Court of Justice held:

> "[W]here a woman is absent owing to illness resulting from pregnancy or childbirth and that illness arose during her pregnancy and persisted during and after her maternity leave, her absence not only during maternity leave but also the period extended from the start of pregnancy to the start of maternity leave cannot be taken into account for the computation of the period justifying her dismissal [on grounds of ill health and incapacity] under national law.
>
> As to her absence after maternity leave, this may be taken into account under the same conditions as a man's absence, of the same duration, through incapacity to work."

This principle has been similarly implemented in Ireland.[12]

As such, the special protection accorded to pregnancy and maternity, as provided under EC and Irish law, cannot prevail for an indefinite period and ceases at a certain point in time. In particular, a female employee is protected throughout her pregnancy, and all the way through to the end of the period of statutory maternity leave. Moreover, a pregnant employee, or an employee suffering from a pregnancy related illness during the course of her pregnancy and statutory maternity leave, cannot be compared to a sick man.

However, an employer may take full account, for the

---

12. *McKenna v. North Western Health Board*, DEC–E2001–025 (See Labour Court decision on appeal).

purposes of its sick leave scheme, of pregnancy related absences occurring after the period of statutory maternity leave. Moreover, after the end of the statutory maternity leave period, an employee who is absent from work due to a pregnancy related illness may be compared with a sick man, and may be treated as a sick man would for an absence from work for a similar period (in other words, the period *after* the end of the statutory maternity leave of the female employee).

Positive action

Thirdly, Article 2(4) of the Equal Treatment Directive does not prohibit measures to promote equal opportunities for men and women in particular by removing existing inequalities which affect women's opportunities.

In *Commission v. France*,[13] this exception was narrowly interpreted. A provision of French law which permitted collective agreements to provide special rights for women in terms, for example, of shorter working hours for older women, and obtaining of leave to care for sick child was not justified under Article 2(4). France had not shown that the "generalised preservation of special rights for women" would reduce actual instances of inequality in social life. Moreover, the European Commission had also condemned them on the ground that evolution of society is such that working men must share the tasks previously performed by women regarding the care and organisation of the family.

Kalanke v. Freie Hansestadt Bremen.[14] Positive action and automatic gender preference: A step too far?

Background This case concerned a German law where if

---

13. [1988] E.C.R. 6315.
14. [1995] E.C.R. 3051.

candidates of different sexes were short listed for promotion and were equally qualified, priority would *have* to be given to a woman where women were under-represented in the job, namely, where women represented less than half the staff.

Findings The ECJ held that since Article 2(4) of the Equal Treatment Directive provided for positive action as a derogation from the principle of equal treatment, it therefore must be strictly interpreted. Therefore, the ECJ said that this law overstepped the limits of the exception in the Directive by making the decision to choose the woman mandatory. In doing so, the ECJ held that it went beyond promoting equal opportunities.

There was much criticism of this decision. As such, a European Commission Communication was issued on the interpretation of the judgment. The Commission took the view that not all quotas were unlawful and also listed a range of permissible positive action measures. It also proposed an amendment to Article 2(4) in the terms that soft quotas were not contrary to the Directive so long as same would *not give automatic preference* to the under-represented sex but permitted assessment of an individual's specific characteristics.

Marschall (Hellmut) v. Land Nor-Rhein-Westfalen.[15] Positive action and soft gender quotas: Getting the balance right

In this case, the ECJ endorsed the above Commission Communication, and held that while a rule guaranteeing absolute and unconditional priority for women was impermissible, a *softer quota* which did allow for consideration of individual circumstances would fall within the existing

---

15. [1997] All E.R. (ECJ) 865.

terms of Article 2(4) of the Directive. Five governments had intervened in this case in favour of positive action.

The ECJ distinguished this case from *Kalanke* on the basis of the fact that the German domestic law impugned in this case contained a saver that, in each case, all the candidates had a guarantee that they would be the subject of *an objective assessment taking account of all criteria specific to the individual* and that this assessment could override the preference given to female candidates where one or more of those criteria tilted the balance back in favour of the male candidate.

As was seen in chapter 3 of this book, paragraph (4) of Article 141 of the EC Treaty now contains a positive action provision with a view to ensuring full equality in practice. It is, however, gender neutral and speaks of the "under-represented sex" rather than women. However, a declaration appended to the Treaty of Amsterdam is material to the interpretation of this issue since it provides for improving the situation of women in working life.

EMPLOYMENT EQUALITY ACT 1998

As such, once again, as with equal pay, in terms of Irish law, equality of treatment is protected under the Employment Equality Act 1998.

What is the meaning of "treatment' under Irish law?

In the first instance, like the above EC law, there is protection against "discrimination", in particular, on the grounds of gender, family and marital status. This is similarly divided between direct and indirect discrimination.[16]

16. This is confirmed by Irish law. See section 22 of the Employment Equality Act 1998 in relation to the definition of indirect discrimination in the context of equal treatment.

In the second instance, there is protection against "sexual harassment." This is a form of sexually motivated and unwelcome pestering or bullying.

In the third instance, there is also protection against "harassment." In this latter case, the offending behaviour may be understood as conduct that, although not offensive or unwelcome in the sexual sense, is offensive, intimidating and unwelcome on, for example, the gender, family or marital status grounds generally. Although the family or marital status grounds of protection are not limited to one particular gender, in that they can apply to men as well as women, the ground of sexual harassment can only be relied upon under Irish law where the harasser is of the *opposite* sex to the victim.

In the final instance, there is protection against "victimisation." The first category of general sex discrimination will be discussed in this chapter. The other three categories of more aggressive sex discrimination will be discussed in chapter 5.

General sex discrimination

The basic test?

Section 6 of the Employment Equality Act 1998 prohibits conduct capable of constituting sex discrimination on a number of fronts. In particular, it states that discrimination occurs when, as between two persons, one person is *treated* less favourably than the other is, has been or would be treated on the ground, *inter alia*, of gender, marital status and family status.

Moreover, every contract of employment (including discriminatory job offers) is now deemed to contain a gender equality clause to give effect to the above provision. This is the case even if the contract is silent in relation to this point. This has the effect of modifying a contract of employment, where it contains a term that discriminates against employees on the gender ground to the extent that it eliminates the discriminatory effect of that term. However, if the difference in treatment is genuinely based on grounds other than sex, then the gender equality does not apply in this regard.[17]

It is also proposed under the Equality Bill 2004 that the 1998 Act will, in future, provide at a new **section 2A** that:

> "Discrimination on the gender ground shall be taken to occur where, on the ground related to her pregnancy or maternity leave, a woman employee is treated, contrary to any statutory requirement, less favourably than another employee is, has been or would be treated."
> (**Section 4(b), Equality Bill 2004**).

Under the Equality Bill, the definition of discrimination is also amended to, interestingly, include the "issue of an instruction to discriminate."[18] Moreover, under the 1998 Act:

(a) An employer shall not discriminate against an employee or a prospective employee in the following terms:
   (i) Access to Employment;
   (ii) Conditions of Employment;
   (iii) Training or Experience for or in relation to Employment;
   (iv) Promotion or Regrading;
   (v) Classification of Posts.

(b) Similarly, an agency employer shall not discriminate against an agency worker in the same terms.[19]

---

17. Section 21 of the 1998 Act.
18. Section 3(a)(i) of the Equality Bill 2004.
19. Section 8 of the 1998 Act.

Trade unions, professional schools and organisations

Moreover, a body which is:

(i) an organisation of workers and employers;

(ii) a professional or trade organization; or

(iii) controls entry to, or the carrying on of, a profession, vocation or occupation

shall not discriminate against a person on the grounds of gender, marital or family status in relation to membership of that body, in relation to the benefits provided by it, in relation to the entry to it or in relation to the carrying on of that profession, vocation or organization (**section 13, 1998 Act**).

Vocational training

The prohibition also extends to training courses designed to prepare a trainee for a profession or trade (vocational training): **section 12(1)**. An educational institution cannot now discriminate against a trainee here also on the grounds of gender, marital or family status:

(i) in the terms on which such course or related facility is offered;

(ii) by refusing or omitting to afford access to any such course or facility to him;

(iii) in the manner in which any such course or facility is provided.

It is also clear from the scope of the 1998 Act that it applies not only to existing employees, but also to prospective employees, in other words, individuals who were subject to discriminatory treatment at the *pre-employment* stage. This most readily applies to the manner in which a job is advertised and the manner in which the interview and selection process for that job is conducted.

Advertising

Under the 1998 Act, advertising relating to employment, and which indicates either an intention to discriminate on the ground of gender or might reasonably be understood as indicating such an intention is now also unlawful: **section 10(1) 1998 Act**.

When the 2004 Equality Bill (as currently drafted at the time of writing) is passed, it is proposed that **section 10(2) of the 1998 Act** will further provide that, for the purposes of section 10(1) of the 1998 Act, where, in an advertisement, a word or phrase is used defining or describing a post and the word or phrase is one which connotes or refers to an individual of one sex, or is descriptive of, or refers to, a post or occupation of a kind previously held or carried on only by individuals of one sex, then, unless the advertisement indicates a contrary intention, it shall be taken as indicating an intention to discriminate on the ground of religion: **section 5, Equality Bill 2004**.

Comparator criteria

Moreover, with some exceptions (particularly in relation to pregnant employees), the definition of discrimination in terms of the *treatment* of individuals, like pay, also necessarily requires a comparison between two persons.

In terms of differences of treatment between two persons, the person with whom an employee may compare him or herself (the "comparator") under the 1998 Act is someone who:

(i) is;

(ii) has been; or

(iii) would be treated differently.

Direct discrimination

Since the definition of discrimination in section 6 of the 1998 Act expressly includes less favourable treatment than another person "*would*" have received, it has been interpreted as specifically permitting the use of hypothetical comparators.[20]

Indirect discrimination

As highlighted at the start of this chapter, the picture is more complex here. In relation to indirect discrimination, the Irish courts have experienced the problem of deciding how necessary it is to have formal statistical proof, in all circumstances, to show that a worker is being discriminated against not just, particularly, as a part-time worker, but more importantly, as a woman.

This problem in practice essentially centres on the nature of the comparison to be made in each case, when such a comparison is required and the extent of the comparator criteria to be used. In a recent case, the Irish Labour Court has gone some way in providing answers to those questions.

Inoue v. NBK Designs Limited:[21] **Part-time work: When the discrimination speaks for itself?**

Background In this Irish Labour Court determination, the complainant was a lone parent, with a schoolgoing child, who commenced work as a part-time secretary/personal assistant in October 2000 in an architectural practice. As part of a job sharing arrangement, another employee would take over from the complainant and carry out the same duties in the afternoon. No criticism attached to the complainant in terms of the

---

20. See below at p.112, *Barry v. Board of Management (Aisling Project), Virgin Mary Schools*, DEC–E2001–E031.
21. [2003] E.L.R. 98.

performance of her duties. Moreover, the inconvenience attaching to the job sharing arrangement was not discussed with the complainant.

Business increased steadily and the respondent decided that it would be more suitable for the business if the two part-time positions were amalgamated into one post. Despite the respondent's awareness of the family commitments of the complainant, she was asked to take the full-time post. Following her refusal to do so, due to her family responsibilities, she was then dismissed.

Submissions An important issue that arose in this case related to whether the complainant was entitled to take for granted, as a female employee, that she was discriminated against on gender grounds, simply because she was also in part-time work which had been cut back. The respondent contended to the Labour Court that since it was a small employer with a limited staff, she should be put on formal proof of this. In other words, she should be required to introduce formal evidence of comparative, statistical data between those of the same sex as herself and those of the opposite sex as to how she claimed she had been discriminated against on the grounds of gender by the simple amalgamation of a part-time job.

However, it was argued on behalf of the complainant that the unequal effect of a requirement to work full-time is so obvious that it should not require formal proof. The Labour Court was also referred to the jurisprudence of the ECJ (as discussed in this book at chapter 3) which is based on the acceptance of the proposition that significantly more women than men are engaged in part-time employment. Finally, it was argued by the complainant that the abolition of a part-time post in favour of a full-time post would impact to a significantly disproportionate degree on women relative to men. As such, it was submitted that it was self-evident that a requirement to work full-time bore more heavily on a woman with child minding responsibilities, particularly lone parents. The complainant also submitted Labour Force Survey data containing statistical information breaking down the structure of the full time and part time work force in terms of gender and family status.

Findings The Labour Court determined that, since its ethos and purpose was to provide redress to workers, howsoever they represented themselves and their resources for same, it would be alien to that ethos to oblige parties to undertake the inconvenience and expense involved in producing elaborate statistical evidence to prove matters which are obvious, by drawing on their own knowledge and experience, to the members of the Court. Furthermore, the Court stated that the official Labour Force survey statistics that were produced by the complainant showed that a significant majority of part-time workers were women, particularly parents of young children and those who are single or separated.

As such, it determined that it may be inferred that the abolition of part-time jobs in a work place would impact disproportionately on women rather than men and, in particular, on women who are lone parents. However, the Labour Court added that the statistics merely provided confirmation based on *the knowledge and experience of its members* of what it understood the position to be.

Furthermore, it also noted that it was clear from the facts disclosed before the Court that the complainant was not able to work full-time not because she was a woman *per se*, but because she was the mother of a school going child, of which she was the primary carer. As such, this was **not** a case of direct discrimination. However, it also noted that it was still the reality in modern society that mothers are more likely to fulfil that role than fathers and where parents were separated or single, it is the mother who was much more likely to have custody of the children.

Consequently, the Court stated that, as a general

proposition, women who have children and who are also single, separated or divorced find it more difficult to find full time work than fathers who are not so single or divorced or who are otherwise not parents. As such, the Court concluded that the elimination of her part-time job indirectly discriminated against the complainant by reference to her gender, family and marital status. Having applied the test for objective justification as set out in *Bilka-Kaufhaus* (see chapter 3), the Labour Court concluded that it could not be objectively justified. The measure taken by the respondent did not correspond to a real need, was not appropriate to achieving its objective and was also not necessary to achieving that end. It awarded the complainant **€1,200**. This comprised of her financial loss when she was out of work and that she had found new employment subsequent to her dismissal. However, it also awarded **€10,000** for the effects of the effects of the discrimination.

As such, having assessed the legal tests and approach to the area of equal treatment, the next issue that may be assessed relates to the various types of conduct and policies that fall foul of this protection.

The scope of the protection?; Access to employment:

Rodmell v. University of Dublin, Trinity College Dublin:[22] *The story of the "Lady Electrician"*

Background This case involved an allegation against the respondent that it had discriminated against the complainant on the grounds of gender in denying her access to employment, contrary to sections 6(2)(a) and 8(1)(a) of the Employment Equality Act 1998.

In particular, in or about August 1999, Trinity College advertised in a number of daily newspapers for suitably

---

22. DEC–E2001–016.

qualified craftspersons for a number of available positions, including that of electrician in the Buildings Office of Trinity. The claimant was the only female candidate invited for interview. There were 18 candidates interviewed.

The complainant alleged that she was discriminated against on the grounds of gender on the basis that, before the interview, she was referred to as a "lady electrician" by a member of the interview board.

The respondent contended that the reference to the "lady electrician" was not discriminatory. It contended that the term was simply used as a means of identifying the candidate from the rest of the other candidates. The respondent further added that the reason why she did not get the post was due to her lack of technical knowledge in areas specific to the post.

Findings The Equality Officer determined that the respondent had discriminated against the claimant.

He found that the fact that since a member of the interview board clearly identified the claimant by her sex, prior to the interview commencing, this was sufficient to constitute discrimination under the Employment Equality Act 1998.

However, with regard to the filling of the vacancy concerned, the Equality Officer found that the Interview Board acted in a non-discriminatory manner in selecting the most suitable candidate for the job and that the formal interview procedure was carried out in a fair and equitable manner.

Nonetheless, the Equality Officer ordered the respondent to pay the claimant **£1,500** in compensation for the distress and humiliation suffered by her as a result of the discriminatory treatment to which she had been subject, prior to her interview, on the grounds of gender. This decision was not appealed.

Wilson v. Adelaide and Meath Hospital:[23] *Collectively agreed discrimination?*

Background This case examined whether industrial relations' considerations could justify indirect gender discrimination. The complainant, a female ward attendant at the hospital, claimed she was discriminated against when she was refused a job as a hospital porter. There had been two competitions in which all the successful candidates were drawn from a pool of temporary porters from the former hospitals, which was exclusively male.

The competitions took place against the background of the relocation and amalgamation of a number of hospitals on a new site. However, union/management negotiations before the relocation had resulted in an industrial relations protocol which effectively provided that staff holding temporary contracts in the former hospitals would be given priority in filling permanent posts as they arose in the new hospital.

In the first competition, all the successful candidates were drawn in accordance with this protocol from this pool of temporary porters from the former hospitals, which was exclusively male. Similarly, the second competition, in which the complainant was unsuccessful, followed the same path and once again drew all the successful candidates from the male ranks of the temporary porters. The complainant had applied for the post together with twelve other candidates. She along with the other candidates had been interviewed for the post. Nonetheless, the jobs went to eight male candidates.

Findings The Labour Court found that the first competition was governed by the custom and practice of the respondent as well as the IR protocol agreed. As such, in recruiting from an exclusively all male pool on the first occasion, the

23. Labour Court, EDA 037.

respondent was simply acting in accordance with its
agreement at the time of rationalisation and there was no
competition in the meaningful sense.

However, the Labour Court found that the second
competition in February 2000 was a different matter. The
complainant was unsuccessful in circumstances where the
respondent had again given priority to an all male pool of
temporary porters, even though these were not now covered
by the original Protocol.

The Labour Court determined that there was no doubt
but that the successful candidates received better treatment
than the complainant. Positions were reserved for the
temporary male candidates while the complainant was
expected to compete with the other four candidates for a place
on a panel only. The complainant was never told that the
nature of the competition in which she was engaged was for
a place on a panel only and that the permanent posts advertised
were filled by automatic selection.

However, the Labour Court determined that this was not
direct discrimination. The difference in treatment related to
the fact that those appointed held temporary posts (and the
industrial significance of that from the perspective of the
respondent). The complainant did not hold a temporary post.
As such, it was a difference unrelated to her sex.

Instead, the Labour Court determined that the conduct of
the competition amounted to *indirect* discrimination on the
basis that the above-mentioned criterion for selection to the
permanent posts was satisfied only by men. As such, the
Labour Court applied the objective justification test.[24] In
doing so, it made the following findings:

> i. The respondent was faced with safeguard-
> ing the competing rights of the temporary

---

24. In particular, the Court applied the precise test set out in chapter 3
of this book arising from the case of *Bilka-Kaufhaus, GmbH v.
Karin Weber Von Hartz* [1986] E.C.R. 1607.

post holders who had a legitimate expectation of obtaining permanent posts and the right of the complainant to equality of opportunity and the right not to be discriminated against.

ii. Faced with those competing rights, it was not open to the respondent to choose arbitrarily between them. The respondent did not consider any options by which the conflict of competing rights might have been avoided.

iii. The difficulties which emerged in the filling of these posts were probably inevitable given the gender imbalance in the temporary porter grade and the established custom and practice used to fill them. This was a difficulty that the respondent should have anticipated.

iv. At a minimum, they could have discussed the matter with the Union of which the complainant and the others affected were members. They could have explored the possibility of obtaining sanction to bring forward the filling of other posts which were subsequently filled.

As such, the Labour Court determined that the conduct of the second competition was not objectively justified and upheld the decision of the Equality Officer, at first instance, directing that the complainant be appointed retroactively to the post. The Labour Court also upheld the Equality Officer direction that the respondent review all its selection and appointment procedures to ensure that they complied with the 1998 Act.

The complainant was awarded **€1,000** to compensate her for the distress suffered as a result of the discrimination.

Barry v. Board of Management (Aisling Project), Virgin Mary Schools:[25] **Discriminatory questions at interview: The cost of getting it wrong**

Background The respondent was a state funded programme involving three schools in the Ballymun area of Dublin. It was designed to provide a home-like setting for selected primary school children to work on homework and socialise after school in a supervised environment. The Board of Management of Virgin Mary Schools was given the task of selecting a Director for the Aisling project which it advertised publicly.

The complainant, who was one of five (all female) candidates called for interview, complained that she was discriminated against because of her gender and marital status when she was asked at interview how she would cope with looking after her family and working full time outside the home.

The complainant was married with children. She was not appointed to the position. However, the appointee was single. She brought a claim under the Employment Equality Act 1977 (relating to acts of alleged discrimination that occurred at periods of time before the enactment into law of the Employment Equality Act 1998) alleging that she had been the subject of discrimination on the gender and marital status ground.

Findings The Equality Officer was satisfied from the evidence, that the Board of Management had discriminated against the complainant on the grounds of her marital and family status.

However, there was no male candidate in the interview process. Nonetheless, the Equality Officer was also satisfied from the evidence that a male candidate would not have been

25. DEC–E2001–E031.

asked the discriminatory question in relation to his family commitments.

The Equality Officer also concluded that the use of a hypothetical male comparator (specifically provided for under the Employment Equality Act 1998) was also permissible under the 1977 Act. As such, the Equality Officer recommended that:

> i.   The respondent pay to the claimant the sum of **£1,000**;
>
> ii. The respondent review its interview process to ensure that discriminatory questioning does not occur again;
>
> iii. The respondent ensure that interview notes for all future vacancies by maintained for a period of at least twelve months after interview.

This decision was not appealed.

Promotions

Lynskey v. Board of Management, Coolmine Community School:[26] **Sex discrimination and the flawed interview process**

Background This dispute concerned a claim by Mr Lynskey, who was employed as a teacher of English and Italian at Coolmine Community School, that the Board of Management discriminated against him on the ground of gender, contrary to the provisions of the Employment Equality Act 1977. He had been unsuccessful in a promotional competition for the post of Deputy Principal.

The claimant alleged that his qualifications, experience

---

26. DEC–E2002–035.

and service rendered him a more suitable candidate than the female appointee. He also argued that there was a "climate of opinion" in the school favouring a female candidate for the post.

The respondent denied that discrimination had occurred and said the onus of proof was on the claimant who had merely made an unsubstantiated allegation.

Findings The Equality Officer was satisfied that an objective assessment of the curriculum vitae of the two candidates prior to interview would conclude that:

> i.   They both reached the minimum academic standard;
> ii. They had at least comparable further qualifications;
> iii. The claimant had more extensive experience than the female employee, both as a teacher and the holder of a post of responsibility.

The Equality Officer further found that the Selection Committee approached the interview without any clear standard for the post to be filled and without any specific or objective criteria against which to measure candidates. The Equality Officer was also satisfied that the Selection Committee;

> i. Was confused regarding the roles of its members during the interviews; and
> ii. It failed to give the claimant credit for certain qualities and experience he patently had.

The Equality Officer concluded that the claimant had established a *prima facie* case of discrimination which the respondent had failed to rebut.

Conclusion The Equality Officer concluded that the respondent had indeed discriminated against the claimant in this case on the ground of gender contrary to the provisions of the Employment Equality Act 1998. She recommended that the claimant be paid the sum of **€5,000** in compensation for the effects of the discriminatory treatment. She also recommended that:

   i. All future interview boards have specific criteria for the post being filled;
  ii. The respondent utilise a formal marking scheme for candidates;
 iii. The respondent retain comprehensive written notes of the interview notes for a period of twelve months following the conclusion of the interview process.

This decision was not appealed.

Tynan v. FÁS[27] **Sex discrimination and the interview board**

Background In this case, the male complainant applied for the post of Manager of Community Services in Programme Development with the respondent. He was successful at the first interview. He was then called to a second interview. At that stage, there were two remaining candidates, a male and a female, who were called to this second interview.

However, the male candidate was unsuccessful and the female candidate was appointed. The complainant claimed that he had more experience in the community sector than the candidate appointed. He alleged that he had been discriminated against on the gender ground. He further alleged that the decision to appoint a female to the post was made in

---

27. DEC–E2002–034.

response to pressure to address the gender imbalance in the respondent, FÁS.

Findings The Equality Officer determined this case in accordance with a number of considerations:

Interview Board and Selection Criteria

i.   The constitution of the interview board was in accordance with its written policy on the matter;

ii. The successful candidate was better qualified than the complainant;

iii. Whilst the complainant may have had more experience in the Community Sector, this was also not a requirement or criteria for appointment to the post.

iv. It was also not a requirement for the promotion that the successful candidate should have experience at Assistant Manager grade within FÁS.

Gender Equality Promotion

The Equality Officer concluded that developing a plan to overcome significant gender imbalances in the gender profile of the respondent was indeed a goal of respondent.

However, the Equality Officer also concluded that there was no policy in this case to promote female staff over male staff. Therefore, there was no reason for her to consider section 24 of the Employment Equality Act 1998, allowing an employer, in accordance with EC law as discussed above, to engage in positive action to promote equal opportunity for men and women.

Conclusion The Equality Officer found that the complainant had failed to establish a *prima facie* case of discrimination. This decision was not appealed to the Labour Court.

Sheehan v. Director of Public Prosecutions:[28] **The glass ceiling and the workplace: can it apply to men?**

Background In this case, the complainant alleged that he had been discriminated against by the Director of Public Prosecutions on the grounds of his gender and age. In particular, he alleged that he was unsuccessful in a competition for appointment to the position of Solicitor in the office of the DPP. The successful candidate was a younger woman with less experience. The complainant said his treatment was in breach of natural justice because of:

    i. A seven year post-qualification experience requirement;
   ii. The behaviour of the respondent prior to the interview process;
  iii. The manner in which the interview was conducted;
   iv. The composition of the Interview Board members;
    v. The alleged improper reference by a Board member to his 'maturity'.

The respondent denied discrimination. It stated that the decision to select another candidate resulted from a *bona fide* assessment by the Board of the relative merits of the complainant and the other candidates. This was based on its consideration of:

    i. The ability of the candidates to meet the

28. DEC–E2002–047.

criteria for the position in accordance with
the job specification and essential requirements of the job;
ii. The curriculum vitae of each candidate;
iii. Their performance at interview.

Findings The Equality Officer determined that the eligibility
criteria are a matter for the respondent employer to establish.
In particular, she also pointed out that the seven-year
experience requirement did not exclude the complainant. She
concluded that the allegations made had not provided
evidence of discrimination on gender or age grounds. Finally,
she determined that the decision relating to who was the most
meritorious candidate was a matter for the Interview Board.
As such, she concluded that the respondent had not
discriminated against the complainant in this case.

Boland v. Eircom:[29] **Refusal of promotion and objective justification: The factors that may be considered**

Background This dispute concerned a claim by Ms Boland
that Eircom discriminated against her on the ground of sex
when she was refused assignments to a higher grade and she
was not permitted to participate in a promotional competition.

The respondent denied the allegation of discrimination.
It said that that the complainant was considered unsuitable
for higher grade assignments because of her lack of
assertiveness and that she was excluded from promotional
competitions because of her sick leave record.

Findings Having considered the undisputed facts, the
Equality Officer was satisfied that the claimant had
demonstrated a *prima facie* case of discrimination and that

---

29. DEC–E2002–019.

the burden of proof had shifted to the employer to show that it had not discriminated against the claimant on objective non-discriminatory grounds.

Assertiveness? In relation to the contention of the respondent that the claimant lacked the assertiveness necessary for assignment to a higher grade, the Equality Officer found that there were no objective reasons for that conclusion.

The only objective assessment of the claimant's performance, which had been carried out in relation to the promotion competition, had found that she had either occasionally or consistently exceeded expectations in all of the core and additional competencies being assessed. Assertiveness was not one of these competencies. As such, the Equality Officer concluded that the respondent had failed to rebut the presumption of discrimination in relation to assignments to the higher grades.

The Equality Officer further found that a personal development plan, proposed by the respondent, as an aid to the claimant's future career development, had been drafted without any knowledge of the claimant's strengths and weaknesses.

She also considered that certain letters sent to the claimant, issued in error by the respondent, demonstrated a casual discourtesy inappropriate for a company dealing with its employees. Finally, she considered that the respondent's lack of any regular appraisal scheme for what it referred to as "graded staff" contradicted best practice in human resource management.

Sick Record? In relation to the claimant's sick record, the Chief Medical Officer (CMO) had indicated no objection to the discounting of absences of two particular illnesses which had required surgery. This was noted by the Equality Officer.

However, the respondent stated that the CMO had been surprised by the length of the claimant's absence on sick leave

FOR USE IN COLLEGE LIBRARY
SOUTH RICHMOND STREET
DUBLIN 2.
PHONE 01-4787667

and he had suggested that there may be a "performance issue." No evidence was produced of this.

The Equality Officer concluded that speculation attributed to the CMO became represented in the internal documentation of Eircom as a statement that the claimant's performance was less than satisfactory. She also noted that later correspondence stated that the CMO had disallowed the discounting on the basis of an unsatisfactory performance.

The Equality Officer concluded that the respondent had no objective basis for this assessment of the claimant's performance and that the decision not to discount the sick leave was based on a serious misrepresentation of the facts.

She concluded that the respondent had failed to rebut the presumption of discrimination in relation to the claimant's exclusion from the promotional competition.

Results of Equality Officer's determination The Equality Officer determined that Eircom had discriminated against the claimant on the grounds of her sex in terms of section 2(a) and contrary to section 3 of the Employment Equality Act 1977. She recommended that the respondent pay the claimant the sum of **€20,000** in compensation for the discrimination suffered by her and that the claimant's sick leave absences relating to specific sick leave absences should not constitute a barrier to her participation in future promotional competitions. She further recommended that the company;

>   i.   Institute a formal appraisal process for all staff;
>   ii.   Line Managers receive specific training in conducting the appraisals;
>   iii.   The Company develop and circulate a comprehensive Equality Policy;
>   iv.   The Company engage the services of Professional Human Resource practitioners to assist in the implementation.

This decision was appealed to the Labour Court.

Appeal to Labour Court: A Salutary Lesson? The respondent appealed this determination of the Equality Officer. The complainant cross-appealed. Not only was the Recommendation upheld in its substance, the Labour Court *increased* the amount of compensation by €4,000. It also **reinforced** the determination of the Equality Officer by recommending the actual appointment of the complainant to the next available acting-up position.

Kennedy v. Thurles Golf Club:[30] *The interview process and assessing the performance of candidates*

Background This case involved bar employees of the respondent club. In April 1999, the complainant and a male candidate were interviewed for the position of Bar Manager. The interview board was comprised of three male members.

The claimant was unsuccessful, and alleged that she had been discriminated against in the selection process on the basis of her gender. She further alleged that she had been victimised for contacting the Employment Equality Authority (the predecessor of the Equality Tribunal) in relation to her equality claim.

In terms of the latter allegation, the claimant contended that the respondent had terminated a payment that it used to make to her for her day off which she had been in receipt of for a considerable period of time. It was also alleged that there had been an attempt to change her staff roster in circumstances that also amounted to victimisation. The respondent denied these allegations.

Findings The Equality Officer found that the claimant

---

30. DEC–E2001–E019.

established a *prima facie* case of gender discrimination on the basis of:

  i.   Her greater Bar experience;
  ii. Her performance of managerial functions on occasion;
  iii. Her performance was at all times satisfactory;
  iv. The all male interview board;
  v.   The lack of transparency in the interview process.

The respondent, in seeking to objectively justify the appointment of the male candidate, relied on:

  i.   The experience of the successful candidate as a Bar Manager;
  ii. His Certificate in supervisory management;
  iii. His performance at the interview was impressive according to the interviewers.

The Equality Officer found that, on the basis of the evidence presented, while the successful candidate was better qualified, it was not clear that he had previously held the position of Bar Manager. There was also a lack of a job specification for this post, of assessment criteria, of a marking system or even notes. As such, the Equality Officer concluded that it was not clear how it could be objectively stated how the interview performance of one candidate was better than the other.

The Equality Officer further concluded that a very selective interview process had operated in this case. As such, in the circumstances, the respondent had failed to satisfy the Tribunal that the selection process was fair, objective and free of any gender bias.

As such, the Equality Officer was satisfied that the respondent had failed to rebut the claim of discrimination and victimisation as alleged. However, interestingly, it was also determined in this case that there was insufficient evidence to conclude that a non-biased selection process operating a non-discriminatory selection process would have concluded that the female candidate was the person for the job.

Recommendations The Equality Officer recommended that:

    i. The respondent pay the claimant the sum of **£5,000** for the distress suffered as a result of the discrimination in the selection process for the Bar Manager interview;

    ii. There be complete transparency in all future selection procedures;

    iii. There be an appropriate gender balance in future interview boards;

    iv. The respondent pay the claimant **£3,000** for the distress suffered as a result of the victimisation occurring before the 18th October 1999.

    v. The respondent liaise with the Equality Authority in relation to the drafting of an Equal Opportunities Policy.

This determination was not appealed.

Terms and conditions of employment.

Roberts v. Dun Laoghaire/Rathdown County Council:[31] Secondment, career breaks and indirect discrimination: Where to draw the line?

Background The complainant alleged that she was directly discriminated against on grounds of her gender when she was refused secondment by her employer in September 2000. She also alleged that she was indirectly discriminated against on the grounds of her gender because secondment was granted to Engineering Staff (who were predominantly male) whereas the clerical grades, including the grade she was serving in, were predominantly female.

Findings The Equality Officer was satisfied that the respondent had introduced restrictions to its career break scheme in May 2000 and that this applied to all staff. He was also satisfied that, in the absence of any specific criteria in respect of secondment, it was reasonable for the respondent to apply the same criteria similar to those operated for career breaks.

The Equality Officer found that all applications for secondment for 1999 and up to May 2000 were approved.

Direct discrimination While two applications received from male employees after May 2000 were approved, the Equality Officer concluded that there were grounds other than gender for the respondent's decision and that she had, therefore, failed to establish a *prima facie* case of *direct* discrimination.

Indirect Discrimination The Equality Officer found that the pool of employees affected after May 2000 by the policy of the respondent to restrict secondment was too small on which to arrive at a conclusion of indirect discrimination.

---

31. DEC–E2002–051.

In this regard, he did accept that, when data relating to the period of May 2000 to April 2002 was examined, it indicated that that 50% of male applications were affected whereas 100% of female applicants were affected. However, this was because it was the complainant herself that comprised the entire female composition of this pool affected.

The Equality Officer concluded that this was insufficient to ground a claim of indirect discrimination.

The Equality Officer concluded that the complainant had failed to establish a *prima facie* case of discrimination. This decision was not appealed.

Weir v. St. Patrick's Hospital:[32] **Refusals to allow job-sharing: A case of the level-playing field?**

Background In this case, the claimant alleged that she was directly and indirectly discriminated against by the respondent on the grounds, *inter alia*, of gender and family status, in terms of section 2(a), 2(b) and 2(c) of the Employment Equality Act 1977.

The application of the complainant to job share in her supervisory position as Deputy Nursing Officer was refused. However, her application for job-sharing would have been granted if she had been willing to revert back to position of staff nurse.

Findings The Equality Officer found that the respondent had not directly discriminated against the complainant in terms of the 1977 Act. The claim in relation to discrimination on the grounds of family status was also similarly rejected.

In terms of indirect discrimination, it was determined that the claimant had discharged the *prima facie* burden of proof that the respondent had a discriminatory policy in place which adversely affected more females than males. Moreover, the

32. DEC–E2001–011.

respondent had failed to objectively justify this policy of not allowing staff at supervisory grades to job share. However, the Equality Officer also determined that this did not mean that all applications for job-sharing by staff at supervisory levels had to be facilitated.

Instead, the respondent had to decide on the suitability of each post for job sharing *by objectively justifying a decision* when it deemed a post unsuitable for job sharing.

The respondent in this case had failed to undertake this exercise in terms of the application of the complainant here for a job-sharing arrangement. In other words, the claimant had no absolute right to job share but the respondent also had a responsibility to objectively justify its decision that no posts at the grade in which the claimant worked was suitable for job sharing.

A failure to do this would mean that there was no reason upon which the respondent could refuse an application to job share.

As such, the Equality Officer concluded that the respondent had indirectly discriminated by having this policy in place.

Conclusions The Equality Officer recommended that:

i.   The respondent examine each post at the claimant's grade and objectively justify its reason for stating that it is unsuitable for job-sharing;

ii. The respondent pay the claimant the sum of **£4,000** (pre-Euro period) to compensate her for the effects of the indirect discrimination.

This decision was not appealed.

Termination of employment

Susan Curran v. Newbridge Credit Union: **Justifying the dismissal of a part-time worker?**[33]

Background This dispute concerned a claim where the complainant was employed as a part-time clerical/administrative worker. She alleged that she had been discriminated against by the respondent on the grounds of gender, marital status and family status when she was denied access to a full-time position.

The claimant contended that she was told that she was being dismissed because the respondent decided to move to a corporate structure of full-time staff. She further complained that she was told that she had not been considered for the post because of her commitment to her school-going children.

The respondent rejected the claim of discrimination against it. It contended that the claimant was dismissed because of problems with her interactions with members and staff at the Credit Union. It asserted that it had not changed its policy with respect to part-time staff and was in fact recruiting for both full time and part time staff at the time of the complainant's dismissal. The respondent also denied that it had made any reference to the complainant's children.

Findings On the basis of the facts submitted at the hearing, the Equality Officer was satisfied that the respondent had presented its concerns relating to certain relationship difficulties to the claimant prior to her dismissal. The respondent also had demonstrated that its recruitment campaign had sought both full time and part time staff.

Staff Profiling The staff profile of the credit union showed that employees were a mixture of:

---

33. DEC–E2002–023.

    i. Male and female;

   ii. Married and single;

  iii. With and Without Children;

  iv. Full and Part Time.

In relation to the serious allegation made in relation to the complainant's commitment to her children, the Equality Officer could not identify from the facts of the evidence presented any plausible context in which the comment as alleged might have been made.

As such, the Equality Officer concluded that the respondent did not discriminate the complainant contrary to the Employment Equality Act 1998.

Therefore, having established the general principles of equal treatment and the protection of the **numerous** different types of conduct that fall within its remit in this chapter, we will now, in the next chapter, look at three particularly aggressive and intimidating forms of sex discrimination, harassment, sexual harassment and victiminisation.

CHAPTER 5

Specific Forms of Aggressive Sex Discrimination

As will be appreciated, sex discrimination is not limited to issues of pay and the more subtle forms of direct or indirect less favourable treatment as already discussed in the course of this book at chapters two, three and four. As well as these types of discrimination, sex discrimination in a workplace can be quite blatant and unapologetic. As such, this chapter deals with this further category of more aggressive, predatory conduct existing in workplaces today and which also may amount to sex discrimination. This further category is a distinct one and may be assessed separately under one or more of the following three headings:

(a) sexual harassment.

(b) harassment.

(c) victimisation.

SEXUAL HARASSMENT

Under the Employment Equality Act 1998 (**hereinafter referred to as the 1998 Act**) Act, sexual harassment occurs where:

– there is any act of physical intimacy by B towards A, or any request by B for sexual favours from A, or any other act or conduct of B (including, without limitation, spoken words, gestures, or the production, display or circulation of written words, pictures or other material);

and

– the act, request or conduct is unwelcome by A **and** could reasonably be regarded as sexually, or otherwise on the gender ground, offensive, humiliating or intimidating to A.[1]

– "A" and "B" represent two persons of the opposite sex so that where "A" is a woman, "B" is a man and *vice versa*.[2]

Same-sex harassment is not covered by this definition. In other words, the harasser must be of the opposite sex to the victim.

The location

An employee may be sexually harassed either:

– **In the workplace**; *or*

– Is subjected **outside the workplace** to work-related harass-ment.[3]

Examples

Physical conduct of a sexual nature

This conduct may include ***unwelcome*** physical contact such as unnecessary:

• touching;

• patting;

• pinching;

• brushing against another employee's body;

---

1. Section 23(3) of the 1998 Act.
2. Section 18(1) of the 1998 Act.
3. Section 23(1) of the 1998 Act.

- assault; *or*

- coercive sexual intercourse.

Verbal conduct of a sexual nature

This includes behaviour such as ***unwelcome***:

- sexual advances;

- propositions;

- pressure for sexual activity;

- continued suggestions for social activity outside of the workplace after it has been made clear that such suggestions are unwelcome;

- unwanted or offensive flirtations and suggestive remarks;

- lewd innuendo and comments.

Non-verbal conduct of a sexual nature

This may include the display of pornographic or sexually suggestive:

- pictures;

- objects;

- written materials;

- e-mails;

- faxes; *or*

- mobile telephone text-messages.

Sex-based conduct

This includes conduct that denigrates, ridicules or is intimidatory or physically abusive of an employee because of his or her gender. This may comprise of derogatory or degrading abuse or insults that are gender-related.[4]

HARASSMENT GENERALLY

Apart from sexual harassment, harassment generally is also unlawful under the 1998 Act. Harassment is any act or conduct including spoken words, gestures or the production, display or circulation of written words, pictures or other material, if the conduct is unwelcome to the employee and could reasonably be regarded as offensive, humiliating or intimidating.[5]

This definition of harassment is the same as that of sexual harassment, but without the sexual element. In other words, an employee may be bullied on the gender, family status or marital status grounds but not to the extent that the unlawful conduct also takes on a sexual element.

Nonetheless, the harassment has to be based on or motivated by the relevant characteristic of the employee targeted. In terms of sex discrimination, the relevant characteristics may be:[6]

(i)   marital status;

(ii) family status;

(iii) gender.

---

4. The above examples are provided in the *Code of Practice on Sexual Harassment and Harassment At Work*, Equality Authority, Dublin 2002.
5. Section 32(5) of the 1998 Act.
6. Section 6(2) of the 1998 Act.

The location

An employee may also be harassed in this way either:

In the workplace; *or*

Is subjected **outside the workplace** to work-related harassment.[7]

Therefore, a wide range of behaviour, when related to one or more of the above three grounds, may constitute harassment. It may include:[8]

• Verbal harassment: Jokes, comments, ridicule or songs.

• Physical harassment: Jostling, shoving or any form of assault.

• Written harassment: Faxes, e-mails, text messages, bulletins or notices.

• Intimidatory harassment: Gestures, posturing or intimidatory poses.

• Isolation or exclusion from social activities.

• Pressure to behave in a manner that the employee thinks is inappropriate.

Both a claim for sexual harassment and harassment (without a sexual element) under the 1998 Act share the same common elements for the purposes of proof and attributing liability.

---

7. Section 32(2) of the 1998 Act.
8. *Code of Practice on Sexual Harassment and Harassment At Work*, Equality Authority (Dublin 2002), pp.8 and 9.

Proving the claim of harassment or sexual harassment

The two ingredients

The test for proving harassment or sexual harassment contains a subjective and an objective element. This means that an employee must show that the conduct is unwelcome **and** is to be reasonably regarded as offensive, humiliating or threatening.[9]

Unwelcome

Each employee must decide:

(a) what behaviour is unwelcome to them, irrespective of the attitude of others to the matter;

(b) from whom, if anyone, such behaviour is welcome or unwelcome, irrespective of the attitude of others to the matter.

The fact that an individual has previously agreed with or acquiesced in the behaviour does not prevent him or her from deciding that it has now become unwelcome.

"Reasonably be regarded"

This is the same test as for bullying dealt with earlier in this Guide. This means that even if the conduct complained of is unwelcome, it must not be so trivial or insignificant that a reasonable, objective employee would not consider it offensive, humiliating or intimidating. Although an employee must decide what is unwelcome, irrespective of the attitude of others, he or she must, nonetheless, cross this threshold before his or her claim is capable of succeeding.

---

9. Section 23(3)(sex harassment) and section 32(5) (harassment) of the 1998 Act.

This helps to protect employers from vexatious claims. It also protects them from claims by employees who may be unreasonably sensitive, conservative or modest. However, as with bullying generally, the employer must be careful not to overlook conduct simply because he himself does not believe it to constitute harassment, if an employee brings it to the attention of the business or complains about it.

Is the intention of the harasser important?

The intention of the perpetrator of the sexual harassment or harassment is not relevant to succeeding in a claim. The fact that an alleged perpetrator did not have the intention of harassing or sexually harassing the employee is not a defence. It is the *effect* of the behaviour on the employee that is important.

The 1998 Act protects employees from harassment and sexual harassment by:[10]

- an employer;

- fellow employees;

- clients of the business;

- customers; *or*

- other business contacts. This includes any person with whom the employer might *reasonably expect* the employee to come into contact with in the workplace.

This may include those who supply or deliver goods or services to the employer, maintenance and other types of professional or trade contractors as well as any volunteers, interns and persons on work-experience.

---

10. Sections 23(1), 32(1), 23(4), 32(2) of the 1998 Act.

THE SCOPE OF THE PROHIBITION

THE SCOPE OF THE PROHIBITION

Location

The scope of sexual harassment and harassment reaches beyond the workplace to work-related events or events that are attended by employees in the course of their employment. Therefore, conferences and training seminars that occur outside the workplace are covered. It may also extend to work-related social events. This may be particularly so if they are arranged and organised officially by an employer.

Different treatment

The protection extends to where an employee is treated differently in the course of his or her employment because he or she has either rejected or accepted the sexual harassment or harassment. Examples of such different treatment may be related to decisions taken concerning the employee's promotion, access to training or salary. Where an employee is treated differently in this way, it constitutes another, fresh act of harassment or sexual harassment.[11]

Other situations covered

As with sex discrimination generally, the law prohibiting harassment and sexual harassment also applies to students or persons in vocational training. It also applies to employment agencies.[12]

---

11. Section 23(2)(b) and section 32(2)(b) of the 1998 Act.
12. Section 32(7) and section 23(6) of the 1998 Act.

WHAT DEFENCES ARE AVAILABLE TO EMPLOYERS?

Obligations of the employer

The 1998 Act requires employers to act in a preventative and remedial way. Under the Act, employers are legally and strictly liable for the harassment, sexual harassment and victimisation carried by any of the persons outlined above. In other words, employers are automatically responsible under the Employment Equality Act 1998 for the acts of their employees. They cannot argue that they are not responsible or that they were not aware of them.[13] However, this is not to say that there are not defences available to employers in relation to this type of behaviour or discrimination.

"Reasonably practicable steps"

It is a defence for an employer to prove that he or she took reasonably practicable steps to prevent:

- the particular employee (or the general category of employees sharing his relevant characteristic) being sexually harassed or harassed; and

- the particular employee (or the general category of employees sharing his relevant characteristic) being treated

---

13. Section 15(1). This is important since there remains doubt, in the absence of this express statutory provision, as to the *degree* to which an employer can be held vicariously liable at common law in the civil courts when their employees conduct themselves in this way at work. For the Irish position, see the High Court judgment of *A Health v. BC and the Labour Court* [1994] E.L.R. 27. For the English position, see the House of Lords' judgment of *Lister v. Hesley Hall and Others* [2001] I.R.L.R. 472. For the legal significance and nature of the Irish and English position on workplace vicarious liability see, Eardly John, *Bullying and Stress in the Workplace, Employers and Employees – A Guide* (1st ed., Firstlaw Publications, Dublin 2002), pp.69–76.

differently in the workplace or in the course of employment, and insofar as any such treatment has already occurred, to reverse its effects.[14]

In practice, in order to rely on this defence, an employer, first of all, will have to show that he or she has comprehensive, accessible, effective policies that focus on prevention, best practice, remedial action and an accessible, effective complaints procedure.

Secondly, the steps taken to put the policies and procedures into real effect will also be taken into account.

An employer will not be able to rely on an excellent policy if it has not been effectively and meaningfully implemented.

RIGHTS AFFORDED AN EMPLOYEE WHO COMPLAINS

Material information

Prior to making a complaint under the 1998 Act, an employee is entitled to seek "material information" from the employer in his or her possession about:

- the alleged acts of sexual harassment or harassment at issue;

- the failure of the employer to deal with them;

- the relevant workplace procedures.

"Material information" means, in particular, all non-confidential information that is reasonable for an employee to require. However, information relating to a particular individual and which so identifies him or her cannot be disclosed without the consent of that individual.[15] Moreover, on the enactment of the Equality Bill 2004 into law,

14. Section 15(3), section 23(5) and section 32(6) of the 1998 Act.
15. Section 76(1), (2) and (3) of the 1998 Act.

information about the scale or financial resources of an employer's business will also be excluded from the definition of "material information" which an employee is entitled to request.[16]

There is no obligation on an employer to comply with this request. However, such inference as may seem appropriate may be drawn by the Director of Equality Investigations, the Circuit Court or the Labour Court for the failure to supply the information. Similarly, if the information supplied by an employer is false or misleading.[17]

The Equality Bill 2004: Reinforcing protection against sexual harassment?

It is proposed to amend the Employment Equality Act 1998 in a number of important respects. These amendments will be important for all future sex discrimination claims taken following the enactment of the 2004 Bill into law. **However, claims instituted and proceeding under the 1998 Act *before* the enactment of the Equality Bill 2004 into law will remain unaffected by the amendments made to the 1998 Act therein and the law as set out above will continue to apply.** It is for this reason that the provisions of the 1998 Act before and after its amendment are included, in order to illustrate the legal situation for both existing and future claims in Ireland.

As stated in chapter 2, at the time of writing, this Bill is currently passing through the Oireachtas. However, the following provisions are incorporated in the Bill as it is drafted.

---

16. See section 28 of the Equality Bill 2004 amending section 76(2)(c) of the Employment Equality Act 1998.
17. Section 81 of the 1998 Act.

Some major amendments

Discrimination: A new subtlety

Under the amended 1998 Act, discrimination shall in future be taken to occur where:

(a) A person is treated less favourably than another person is, has been or would be treated in a comparable situation on the [gender, family status or marital status grounds] which:

  (i)   exists;
  (ii) existed but no longer exist;
  (iii) may exist in the future;
  (iv) is imputed to the person concerned.

or

(b) A person who is associated with another person:

  (i) is treated, by virtue of that association, less favourably than a person who is not so associated is, has been or would be treated in a comparable situation on the ground, *inter alia*, of gender, marital status and family status.

Harassment and sexual harassment

The provisions of the 1998 Act **as set out above** and previously dealing with the issues of sexual harassment and harassment are to be deleted. Instead, the Equality Bill 2004 proposes that the test for sexual harassment and harassment in future will be dealt with together in **a new section 14A of the Employment Equality Act 1998** and follow a number of steps:

Step One

(a) An employee is harassed or sexually harassed either at a place where the employee is employed ('the workplace') or otherwise in the course of his or her employment by a person who is:

   (i) employed at that place or by the same employer;

  (ii) the victim's employer;

 (iii) a client, a customer or other business contact of the victim's employer and the circumstances of the harassment are such that the employer ought reasonably to have taken steps to prevent it.

(b) In particular,

   (i) such harassment has occurred:

  (ii) either:

    (I) when the victim is treated differently in the workplace or otherwise in the course of his or her employment by reason of the rejecting or accepting the harassment; or

   (II) when it could reasonably be anticipated that he or she would be treated,

the harassment or sexual harassment constitutes discrimination by the victim's employer in relation to the victim's conditions of employment.

Step Two

If harassment or sexual harassment of the victim by a person other than his or her employer would be regarded as discrimination by his or her employer, it is a defence for the employer to prove that the employer took such steps as are reasonably practicable:

(a) to prevent *this other person* from harassing or sexually harassing the victim or any class of persons which includes the victim, and

(b) to prevent *the victim* from being treated differently in the workplace or otherwise in the course of the victim's employment and, if and so far as any such treatment has occurred, to reverse its effects.

Step Three

A person's rejection of, or submission to, harassment or sexual harassment may not be used by an employer as a basis for a decision affecting that person.

Step Four

The reference to a client, customer or other business contact of the victim's employer includes a reference to any other person with whom the employer might reasonably expect the victim to come into contact in the workplace or otherwise in the course of his or her employment.

Step Five

The meaning of "employee" includes:

(a) a person seeking or using any service provided by an employment agency; and

(b) a person participating in a vocational

training course or facility.

Accordingly, any reference to the individual's employer includes a reference to the employment agency providing the service or, as the case may be, the person offering the vocational training course or facility.

Step Six

(a) (i). References to harassment under this new legislation are to any form of unwanted conduct related to any of the discriminatory grounds; and

(ii). References to sexual harassment under this new legislation are to any form of unwanted verbal, non-verbal or physical conduct of a sexual nature,

being conduct which in either case has the purpose or effect of violating a person's dignity and creating an intimidatory, hostile, degrading, humiliating or offensive *environment* for the person.

(b) Such unwarranted conduct may consist of acts, requests, spoken words, gestures or the production, display or circulation of written words, pictures or other material. (**Section 8 of the Equality Bill 2004**).

Legal disputes: Who decides?

Victimisation

Dismissal

It is a separate criminal offence under the 1998 Act to dismiss an employee for making a complaint of sexual harassment or harassment in good faith. On conviction for this victimisation, the employer may be subject **either** to an award of compensation (on top of any amount awarded for the earlier act(s) of harassment) **or** to orders of reinstatement or re-engagement. A court fine will also be imposed on conviction, and this is irrespective of whether the court makes any order of compensation.[18]

Other penalisation

The 1998 Act also protects employees who seek redress under the Act, or who give evidence in such proceedings from being victimised by dismissal or *by other penalisation other than dismissal* for so doing either during the proceedings or afterwards.[19]

Compensation awards for victimisation have proved very substantial and will continue to do so.

Employers should be particularly vigilant of this protection and ensure that nothing is said or done, as far as is reasonably practicable, that could be interpreted by an employee as victimisation in any way.

What the courts say

As a result, it is of immense importance for employers to be aware of the types of treatment of employees that may lead to claims of victimisation. For example, if there are *genuine redundancies* to be made in the business in a period after any employee has taken a claim or acted as a witness against the employer, that employer must ensure that the selection of that employee for redundancy is scrupulously fair and is capable of being so demonstrated if needs be.

In simple terms, it is also important for employers to know

---

18. Section 98 of the 1998 Act.
19. Section 74(2) of the 1998 Act.

where they can draw the line safely in their dealings with such employees.

There is no definition of the term "*other penalisation*" in the 1998 Act and this comes down to a case-by-case basis. Furthermore, the only real guidance provided in the Act is that the victimisation must be *solely or mainly* occasioned by an employee being involved in proceedings against his employer, in one of the ways specified and protected, under the Act.[20] This fails to deal with many of the practical problems that employers may be faced with, in dealing with staff, rosters and the terms and conditions of work not only after the hearing, but also before and during the proceedings themselves when there has not yet even been any adverse finding made against an employer! For small businesses, this is of particular seriousness. However, two important decisions have recently provided further guidance on these points.

I. In the course of proceedings

Firstly an English House of Lords decision, although not dealing with sex discrimination directly, has confirmed that not every instance of adverse treatment or "*penalisation*" arising out of the course of litigation may necessarily be punishable by the courts. The case involved the refusal of an employer to give his employee a reference pending the outcome of proceedings against him. The entitlement of an employer to do this in Ireland is expressly protected under the 1998 Act and this is not why the decision is important.[21] It is important because it is the most recent affirmation by the Law Lords that certain acts taken by an employer solely to preserve his legal position pending the conclusion of litigation may not automatically be considered as '"victimisation."

---

20. *Ibid.*
21. Section 76(4) of the 1998 Act.

Chief Constable of West Yorkshire Police v. Khan. **Victimisation: In search of the missing link?**[22]

The House of Lords, interpreting the specific definition of "victimisation" under the UK Race Relations Act 1976, held that:

• Employers ought to be able to take steps to protect their positions in pending discrimination proceedings without laying themselves open to a charge of victimisation.

• A test that is likely, in most cases, to give the right answer is to ask whether the employer would have refused such a request if the litigation had been concluded, whatever the outcome. If the answer is no, then it will usually follow that the reason for the refusal was not to victimise an employee.

• On the other hand, if the fact that an employee had commenced proceedings under the Act was *the real reason* why he received less favourable treatment, then it is no answer to such a charge that an employer would have behaved in the same way towards some other employee who had never taken a claim against him.

The importance of this decision does not so much depend on the interpretation and application given to the particular piece of English statute but rather on the general principles and *the reasoning* outlined by the House of Lords in deciding what is appropriate conduct in dealing with employees in the course of proceedings. Such principles equally have a bearing on the definition of "victimisation" in Ireland since, although derived from differing statutory sources and conditions, concrete examples are provided, in cases such as this, as to the grounds on which conduct may be condemned as penalisation under the Irish 1998 Act.

---

22. [2001] I.R.L.R. 830 (December).

The lessons Actions taken by employers, specifically and solely to protect their legal positions and to avoid prejudicing their case, pending the outcome of such litigation, may not automatically fall within the scope of victimisation. However, this is always going to be a matter of fact to be proved by an employer at the hearing of the substantive claim and further guidance will be required from the courts and industrial tribunals to provide a more complete and certain picture on this point.

Nonetheless, it **always** remains the case that if the motivation of an employer is **to punish** an employee for taking the litigation, any acts on foot of this will be considered as penalties. Moreover, where the employee is merely a witness to proceedings or has given notice of same, as is also protected in the 1998 Act, such arguments could never be successfully relied upon.[23] Similarly, after the proceedings are ended, an employer must ensure to avoid any behaviour or alterations capable of being considered victimisation.

In other words, employers should always avoid putting themselves in the position where any such charge may be made against them.

As the next case shows, the consequences of failure are both serious and potentially very expensive.

II. In the aftermath of proceedings

The second case is an Irish determination of an Equality Officer in 2001.

McCarthy v. Dublin Corporation. Sharpening the blades of anti-victimisation![24]

The claimant had previously brought a claim of discrimination

---

23. Section 74(2)(b) and (c) of the 1998 Act.
24. [2001] E.L.R. 255. See also the decision of *Murphy v. Dublin City Council*, DEC–E2002–031.

against her employer, Dublin Corporation before the Labour Court in December 1996. The claimant, a legal assistant, employed by the respondent had been successful in an earlier sex discrimination action due to its failure to promote her to the post of senior legal assistant. The following instances of victimisation were identified by the Equality Officer:

- Since the date of the previous claim, her immediate manager, the Chief Clerk, had ignored her for a period of three years from September 24, 1997 until his departure from the employment of the respondent October 9, 2000.

- The In-house newsletter, *Forum*, distributed widely within the offices of Dublin Corporation had misrepresented the results of the discrimination claim and, despite her written requests to the City Manager, the publication had not been corrected.

- A subsequent bullying complaint had been made *against* her. The internal investigation into that complaint had been conducted contrary to fair procedures and natural justice.

- The claimant had been socially isolated at work since she had referred her original claim of discrimination.

- Despite repeated complaints by the claimant about these incidents of victimisation, no action was ever taken by the respondents.

Decision The decision found that the claimant had been victimised contrary to the 1998 Act. She was awarded compensation in the amount of £40,000 by the Equality Tribunal. This decision was appealed to the Labour Court and the award was reduced to **€25,000**. This was because the Labour Court determined that the Respondent had not victimised the complainant by deviating from fair procedures. There was one exception: the investigators had gone too far in recommending disciplinary action rather than referring the matter back to the Personnel Officer.

On this matter, the Labour Court determined that the disciplinary hearing be reconstituted *de novo*. Moreover, the Labour Court further upheld the entitlement of the Personnel Officer to decide on disciplinary action as an appropriate function in this case. Therefore, it entirely rejected any suggestion that his involvement in the disciplinary process was an act of penalisation or victimisa-tion of the claimant simply because of her earlier allegation of misrepresentation by that officer of the outcome of her earlier proceedings in the "Forum" magazine.

Some important conclusions The Equality Officer and the Labour Court concluded in their determination that the effect of such victimisation is to undermine the entire purpose and effectiveness of the legislation and is completely un-acceptable. Therefore, it will always be dealt with severely.

The Equality Officer stated that the mere adoption of a policy was insufficient unless it was brought to the attention of staff and a consciousness was created in all employees as to what constituted discrimination. This means that simply adopting Equality Policies and an anti-discrimination/harassment policy will not be enough for an employer in order to meet his statutory obligations.

Finally, what is interesting and of much importance is the fact that both the Equality Officer and the Labour Court expressly applied the common law test of vicarious liability as well as the 1998 Act directly to the instances of victimisation complained of in holding the respondent employer responsible. Both had to be applied simply because many of the instances of victimisation complained of related to periods prior to the introduction of the 1998 Act which creates the automatic or "strict'" liability of employers for offences. However, the Equality Officer had no difficulty in holding that acts of victimisation may be carried out within the scope of employment. In particular, she determined that:

- The respondent was vicariously liable both at common law and under statute for the victimisation of the claimant as a result of the Chief Clerk refusing to speak to her.

- The respondent was vicariously liable at common law for the inaccurate reporting at management meeting and the publication afterwards of the decision of her earlier discrimination claim and for the failure to correct the error. In so doing, those involved had acted within the scope of their employment.

Therefore, having set out the many pitfalls that an employer may face, particularly in relation to more direct forms of discrimination such as sexual harassment, in the next chapter, the practical steps that may be taken to avoid such pitfalls are now discussed.

CHAPTER 6

Practical Ways to Prevent Sex Discrimination at Work

GUIDANCE ON THE PREPARATION OF THE EQUALITY POLICY

In short, when it comes to sex discrimination, prevention is better than cure. In this final chapter, we will deal with the issue of the practical steps that employers and employees can take when confronted with instances of sex discrimination in the Irish workplace. While every case is different and some forms of sex discrimination may be more endemic than others, the purpose of this chapter is to outline best practice in the area of employment equality procedures, particularly in situations where the need to deal with a problem is now placed, at first instance, firmly on the shoulders of employers.

Moreover, although aspects of these equality procedures may be most readily invoked in cases involving sexual harassment or bullying at work, they are equally amenable, where appropriate, to dealing with more general issues of equal pay and treatment grievances. However, in the latter cases, concerning issues, for example, of equality of pay or promotion between the genders, an employee's entitlement to equality is non-negotiable and should be implemented from the outset rather than being considered a "grievance" to be processed internally in the workplace. However, for an employer who wishes to avoid the numerous legal minefields outlined in this book, it is always useful to have an effective and fully functioning Equality Policy in the event that grievances, howsoever arising, might be dealt with other than through litigation.

In the first instance, employers should adopt, implement and monitor a comprehensive, effective and accessible policy on workplace, gender-related discrimination, sexual harassment and harassment.

The policy dealing with the prevention of workplace sex discrimination should be produced following consultation with the safety and employee representatives. A policy is most likely to be effective when it is jointly agreed between the employees or their representatives and the employer as a shared sense of responsibility is important in the development of employment equality culture.[1]

The policy and complaints procedure should also, where appropriate and as far reasonably practicable, be adopted after consultation and negotiation with clients, customers and other business contacts or their representatives about its contents and implementation.

It should be written, dated and signed by the employer or his senior management (depending on the size of the business) and updated when appropriate. The language used in the Policy should be simple and direct. It should be accessible to employees with literacy problems and to those who do not speak fluent English.

It should be made available to all staff and highlighted as part of the induction process. It should also be publicised among existing staff on an ongoing basis.

The Employment Equality/Anti-Discrimination Policy must incorporate the following terms in order for it to be considered effective.[2]

---

1. Section 13 of the Safety, Health and Welfare at Work Act 1989 also provides that consultation in this way is a statutory duty.
2. FACTS, European Agency For Safety and Health at Work, Fact sheet, No.23, Belgium 2002; *Code of Practice on Sexual Harassment and Harassment At Work*, Equality Authority, Dublin 2002 (as effected by S.I. No.78 of 2002); *Code of Practice on the Prevention of Workplace Bullying* (HSA) (Dublin, 2002).

The core elements and implementation steps

1. The policy should begin by declaring:

(a) The commitment of the business to ensuring that the workplace is free from discrimination, sexual harassment and harassment.

(b) That all employees have a right to be treated with dignity and respect.

(c) The dedication of the employer to equality of opportunity in the workplace, including in relation to access to and promotion within the business.

(d) That complaints by or grievances of employees will be treated with fairness and sensitivity and in as confidential a manner as is consistent with a fair investigation.

(e) That, in the event of a complaint of discrimination, sexual harassment/harassment being upheld against *employees*, that action will be taken to reverse the effects of same and/or, if appropriate, the disciplinary process will be invoked which may include disciplinary action up to and including dismissal. In the event of a complaint being upheld against *non-employees*, appropriate sanctions may be imposed which could, in particular circumstances, include the termination of contracts, suspension of service or an exclusion from the premises as appropriate.

(f) That using the Complaints Procedure does not affect the Complainant's *statutory rights* to make a complaint under the statutory mechanisms such as the Employment Equality Act and it should specify the statutory time limits.

(g) That in the course of investigating any complaints of a breach of the policy, the employer will make no assumptions about the guilt of the alleged harasser.

(h) That, in the adoption and in the implementation of the Policy, all due regard is accorded to developments in best practice and, in particular, the:

> *Code of Practice on the Prevention of Workplace Bullying* (2002);
> *Code of Practice on Sexual Harassment and Harassment in the Workplace* (2002);
> *Code of Practice Detailing Procedures for Addressing Bullying in the Workplace (2002).*

2. Definitions

(a) The Policy should set out the definitions of discrimination, sexual harassment and harassment that are simple, clear and practical. In particular, it should clarify that:

- A claim for discrimination and harassment must be based on one of nine specified grounds (including gender, marital and family status), sexual harassment relates to the gender ground and bullying generally can include any inappropriate behaviour that may reasonably be regarded as an affront to dignity.[3]
- Acts of bullying not linked on one of the nine grounds is not covered by the Employment Equality Act 1998.
- An isolated, once-off incident of inappropriate behaviour, although an affront to dignity, is not considered bullying for the purposes of a valid complaint, whereas a single act of unwelcome behaviour may constitute a valid complaint of sexual harassment/harassment.

---

3. For a detailed legal assessment of "bullying" in the workplace, see Eardly John, *Bullying and Stress in the Workplace, Employers and Employees – A Guide* (1st ed., Firstlaw Publications, Dublin 2002).

(b) A non-exhaustive list of examples of the different varieties of discrimination, harassment and bullying should be provided. (A comprehensive number of such examples in the context of sex discrimination have been provided in earlier chapters ranging from unequal pay to sexual harassment).

(c) The Policy should state that the protection extends to:

- Discrimination, bullying, sexual harassment/ harassment by co-workers, clients, customers and other business contacts;
- Beyond the workplace to conferences and training and may extend to work related social events;
- Different treatment of an employee because he/she has rejected or accepted the sexual harassment/ harassment;
- In the case of discrimination, sexual harassment/ harassment, employment agencies and vocational training.

(d) The Policy should emphasise that it is up to an employee to decide what is unwelcome or offensive behaviour, irrespective of the attitude of others.

(e) The Policy should state that employees who make a complaint or who give evidence in proceedings will not be victimised.

3. Allocation of responsibilities under the Act

The Policy should state that management and others in positions of authority have a particular responsibility to ensure that discrimination, sexual harassment/harassment does not occur and that complaints are addressed speedily. The Policy should state that, in particular, management should:

(a) provide good example by treating all in the workplace with courtesy and respect;

(b) promote awareness of the business' policy and complaints procedure;

(c) be vigilant for signs of discrimination and harassment and take action before a problem escalates;

(d) respond sensitively to an employee who makes a complaint of discrimination or harassment;

(e) explain the procedures to be followed if a complaint is made;

(f) ensure that an employee making a complaint is not victimised for doing so;

(g) monitor and follow up a situation after a complaint is made so that the discrimination, sexual harassment/ harassment does not recur.

4. *Trade Unions*

The Policy should address the contribution to be made by the trade union(s).

Trade Unions play an important role in prevention and in providing information, advice and representation to both the employees who have made a complaint and to the employees against whom a complaint is made.

5. *Employees*

The Policy should make it clear that employees can contribute to achieving a discrimination and sexual harassment/ harassment free environment through co-operating with management and trade union strategies to eliminate discrimination and harassment. It must also make clear that discrimination and sexual harassment/harassment by employees constitute misconduct and may lead to disciplinary action.

6. Non-employees

The Policy should point out that discrimination, sexual harassment and harassment by non-employees such as clients, contractors and other business contacts will not be tolerated and may lead to the termination/non-renewal of contracts, the suspension/non-renewal of services, exclusion from the premises or the imposition of other appropriate sanctions (depending on the circumstances of the business).

7. Communication of the policy

The Policy should include a commitment to its effective communication. It should be communicated effectively to all those potentially affected by it, in particular, management, workers, customers, contractors and business contacts including those who supply and receive goods and services.

This effective means of communication should include: newsletters, training manuals, training courses, leaflet drops, websites, e-mails, notice boards and staff meetings.

To Employees:

Employees, including those in management and all other positions of responsibility, should be made aware of the Equality Policy as part of any formal induction process to their new job and working environment along with the other health and safety rules and regulations.

Employers are advised to consider a staff handbook where reasonably practicable to be distributed to all employees as part of the induction process. Such a handbook should be kept under on-going review to reflect developments.

To Non-Employees:

No Ongoing relationship: There may be practical difficulties in ensuring that the policy is effectively communicated to every relevant non-employee particularly where there is no ongoing relationship with the business. However, it is advised that summaries of policies should be displayed prominently in the workplace to which these non-employees have access. This should contain a short statement confirming the policy's existence and the business' commitment to it. It should also state that the complete policy is available on request. This type of approach is appropriate to alert the general public of the policy as they avail of certain types of general services from the business. For example, public houses or restaurants.

Ongoing relationship: Where there is an ongoing relationship with customers and clients, the effective communication of the policy is easier to achieve. A number of means may promote this aim:

- Leaflets summarising the policy being prominently displayed in areas where members of the public, clients and customers attend such as receptions and waiting rooms.
- Include a leaflet or short written summary of the Policy in any of the business' brochures.

It may even be appropriate for the contracts of the employer with customers, contractors or other business contacts to expressly include a term providing that the discrimination, sexual harassment/harassment of the employees of the employer will constitute a repudiation of the contract and may be a ground for the employer to terminate the contract.

It has been the tradition of the courts to imply terms into private contracts by analogy with statutes applicable in the same area. Similarly, in the future, in any contractual dispute on this basis, it may also be the case that the courts will imply such a term into all relevant contracts by analogy with the statutory duties of employers now under the 1998 Act.[4]

8. *Monitoring*

The Policy should incorporate a commitment to monitoring incidents of discrimination, sexual harassment and harassment.

This is particularly important in the context of an employer seeking to minimise his legal exposure to litigation. The only way that a business can know if its policy and procedure are working is to keep careful track of all complaints of discrimination and sexual harassment/harassment and how and when they are resolved.

The monitoring information should be used to evaluate the policy and procedures at regular intervals with alterations and improvements made if there is some weakness identified in the system.

9. *Training*

The Policy should contain a commitment to train all staff on issues of Equality and the prevention of sexual harassment/harassment.

An important means of ensuring that discrimination and harassment does not occur is through the provision of training for managers, supervisors and all staff. This should happen for staff at induction or through appropriate awareness raising initiatives.

Such training should aim to **identify** the factors that contribute to a workplace free of discrimination and harassment, to **familiarise** participants with their responsibilities and to **inform** them of any problems they are likely

---

4. McMahon and Binchy, *The Law of Torts* (3rd ed., Butterworths, Ireland 2000), p.488.

to encounter under the Policy e.g. the meaning of the words "unwelcome" or "reasonably be regarded."

10. The complaints' procedure

The Policy should set out a complaints procedure.

This should be attached to the policy. Clients, contractors or business contacts who interact on a frequent basis with the business should be made aware of the employees' right to make a complaint and that they may be requested to participate in the process. The issue of the complaints procedure is discussed on page 161.

11. Review

The Policy should include a commitment to review it on a regular basis in line with changes in statute, case law or other developments

A competent person should be designated to ensure that such monitoring, training and reviews occur.

12. Victimisation

The Policy should guarantee an employee invoking the complaints procedure will be not be victimised or subject to sanction for making a complaint in good faith, for giving evidence in proceedings arising out of it or for giving notice to do so. The effective implementation of an Anti-Discrimination/Harassment Policy requires a reprisal free environment.

13. Counselling service

The Policy should include details as to any counselling and support services available for victims and perpetrators and how to contact them. This information should also come with the assurance of absolute privacy and confidentiality.

The Anti-Discrimination/Harassment policy should be incorporated as a part of the contract of employment of each employee.

THE COMPLAINTS PROCEDURE: ARE YOU KEEPING UP WITH THE LATEST BEST PRACTICE?

As discussed in Chapter 2 of this book, since March 2002, new formal streamlined procedures have been introduced and recommended by the relevant State agencies for implementation with the purpose of addressing sexual harassment and gender-related harassment in the workplace. These are contained in the *Code of Practice Preventing Harassment and Sexual Harassment At Work*. Moreover, they have legal status and are admissible in court. Indeed, in deciding sexual harassment/harassment claims, a court or tribunal must take into account the Code of Practice on Harassment if it is relevant to any issue before it. Therefore, it is vital that employers are aware of the procedures recommended under these Codes and as far as possible adopt and implement them as part of their own anti-bullying/harassment system at work.

Moreover, for those many employers who may already have anti-bullying/harassment procedures in place, it is also important that existing procedures are kept under on-going review to ensure their adequacy and effective implementation. Therefore, it may be worthwhile to test the adequacy of any existing procedures by now comparing them with those recommended in this chapter. It is important that employers be aware that not only is it good practice for them to implement and keep up to date with these procedures, as already discussed, it is also an important factor in determining their exposure to compensation claims in any future litigation. The effective incorporation and implementation of the new procedures will be a factor to which a court or tribunal will, in the future, have serious regard in the event of any claim against an employer.

The **Code of Practice of 2002** provide for a double layered procedure. There is the informal procedure and the formal procedure.

Informal procedure

On many occasions, the recipient of sexual or gender-related harassment simply wants it to stop allowing him or her to get on with the job. As such, an informal approach may be the better way to resolve an issue of sex discrimination in the workplace in the first instance. It is always beneficial to attempt to find a non-confrontational solution before undertaking the formal, more legalistic route. After all, the smaller the workforce, the closer the inter-relationship between all the parties in the workplace and the more likely it is that the parties concerned may have to work together again there. It also minimises the conflict, stress and distress to which a complainant may be already subject:

A. Any employee who feels that he or she is being discriminated against or harassed should object to the conduct where this is possible and appropriate. In many cases, this may be sufficient. He should **explain clearly** to the alleged perpetrator(s) engaging in the unwelcome or offensive behaviour in question that it is unwelcome or that it offends him and that it interferes with his work.

In circumstances where the employee finds it difficult to approach the alleged perpetrator(s) directly, he should seek help and advice, on a strictly confidential basis, from **a contact person**. A contact person could be one of the following:

- a supervisor or line manager;
- any manager in the workplace;

- human resource/personnel officer;
- another employee/Trade Union Representative;

In this situation, it is advised that the contact person listen patiently, be supportive and discuss the various options open to an employee.

B. Having consulted with the contact person, the complainant may request the assistance of the contact person **in raising the issue** with the alleged perpetrator(s). In this situation, the approach of the contact person should be by way of a non-confrontational calm confidential discussion with a view to resolving the issue in an informal, low-key manner.

C. However, a complainant employee may decide and is entitled to bypass, for whatever reason, this informal approach. **Choosing not to use the informal procedure should not reflect negatively on a complainant during the formal process**.

NOTE: It is important for employers, line managers and HR personnel to note the simple point that they themselves, if they become aware of a problem or when they receive a complaint, should not 'jump the gun' for whatever reason and institute the formal procedure without giving *the complainant* him/herself the full opportunity to choose. Employers moving straight into a formal procedure when the complainant may have been satisfied by an informal approach may actually constitute a ground of harassment or victimisation of the alleged bully by the employer!

The formal procedure

If an employee believes that an informal approach is inappropriate, if the discrimination or gender-related harassment is too serious for informality or if, after the informal stage, the sex discrimination persists or re-commences, the formal procedures should be invoked. Under this Procedure:

Part One: The Making and Receipt of the Complaint

A. The complainant should make a formal complaint in writing to his or her immediate supervisor, or if preferred, any member of management. **The complaint should be confined to precise details of the actual incidents of sex discrimination**.

B. The alleged perpetrators should be notified in writing that an allegation of bullying has been made against him or her. He or she should be given a copy of the complainant's statement and advised that **he or she shall be afforded a fair opportunity to respond to the allegation(s)**.

C. The complainant should be subject to **an initial examination by a designated member** of management who is considered impartial with a view to determining an appropriate course of action.

An example of an appropriate course of action at this stage might be exploring the acceptability of **a mediated solution** or a view that the issue might still be resolved informally.

Should either of these approaches be deemed inappropriate or inconclusive, **a formal investigation of the complaint should take place** with a view to determining the facts and the credibility or otherwise of the allegation(s).

Part Two: The Investigation

D. The investigation should be conducted by either a

designated member(s) of management or, if deemed, appropriate, an agreed third party.

It is suggested that at least two people should investigate a complaint with a gender balance and diversity across the other eight grounds in the 1998 Act. However, it is accepted that this may be impractical on occasion.

Nevertheless, in all circumstances, the investigation should be conducted thoroughly, with sensitivity, utmost confidentiality and good faith and with due regard to the rights of both the complainant and the alleged perpetrator(s). The investigation should be, and perceived to be, independent and objective. Those conducting it should not be connected with the allegations in any way.

E. The investigation should be governed by terms of reference, preferably agreed between the parties, or their legal advisers, in advance. The terms of reference must always include the following;

- what this formal procedure provided here involves and the relevant time limits (if not agreed);
- that both parties have the right to be accompanied and/or represented;
- that the alleged perpetrator(s) is to be given full details in writing not only of the nature of the complaint but also all other relevant written statements and any other documentation or evidence including witness statements, interview notes or records of meetings held with the complainant and witnesses relating to the complaint.
- that the alleged perpetrator will be given reasonable time to consider the documentation and an opportunity to respond.

PORTOBELLO COLLEGE LIBRARY
SOUTH RICHMOND STREET
DUBLIN 2.
PHONE 01-4787667

- that the alleged perpetrator(s) is or is not being afforded a full oral hearing in order to cross-examine the complainant and, if so, the date, location and procedure for same.

F. The investigator(s) should then meet with the complainant and the alleged perpetrator(s) and any witnesses or relevant persons on a one-to-one confidential basis with a view to establishing the facts surrounding the allegations. Both the complainant and the alleged perpetrator(s) may, at this point, be accompanied by a legal representative or a work colleague or an employee/trade union representative, if so requested.

G. Every effort should be made to carry out and complete the investigation as quickly as possible and preferably within any agreed time frame. On completion of the investigation, having duly considered all the evidence and representations submitted, the investigator(s) should produce a written report for management containing the findings of the investigation.

H. The complainant and alleged perpetrator(s) should be informed of the findings of the investigation.

I. Both parties should be given the opportunity to comment on the findings before any action is decided upon by the employer or management. Such comments should be duly considered.

Part Three: The Outcome

J. Should management decide that the complaint is well founded against an *employee*, it will be necessary to decide whether the disciplinary procedures of the business should be invoked. The perpetrator should be given a formal interview to determine an appropriate course of action. Such action could involve, as an example, counselling and monitoring or the bringing of the issue through the disciplinary and grievance procedure of the employment.

K. Should management decide that the complaint is well founded against a *non-employee*, it will be necessary to decide what sanctions to enforce against him or his employer. This could extend, where appropriate, to:

- The exclusion of the individual from the premises;
- The suspension or termination of a contract with him;
- The suspension or termination of a service supplied by or to him.

L. The management decision may also, or as an alternative, recommend other actions such as the more effective promotion of the business' policy on sex discrimination, sexual harassment/harassment or training.

If a right of appeal exists both parties should be informed of it and the time limits and procedure involved. If either party is unhappy with the outcome of the investigation, the issue may be processed through the normal industrial relations mechanisms.

Non-employees

It is probable that if the person accused of the sex discrimination such as sexual or gender-related harassment is not an employee, he or she will not wish to participate in the formal procedure and, it will not be possible to secure their participation.

Nonetheless, a non-employee must be kept informed of all developments and given the opportunity to respond to them. The outcome of the investigation and any potential sanctions must also be explained to the non-employee and/or any person or company for whom he/she works.

Confidentiality

All individuals involved in the procedures should maintain confidentiality on the subject.

Training and awareness raising

The Health and Safety Authority (HAS) considers that all personnel with a role in both the formal and informal procedures should be made aware of the appropriate policies and procedures and should, if possible, include appropriate training. An example of such relevant persons would be:

- designated members of management;
- worker representatives;
- "*contact persons*";
- union representatives.

However, an employer should consider what other persons may be considered for such treatment in his or her workplace.

Furthermore, as with the Policy, the Anti-Discrimination/ Harassment Procedure should be incorporated as an express term of the contract of employment to which all employees and the employer must agree, including the specified penalties, suspensions (with or without pay) and other possible sanctions that may arise from a finding of wrongdoing up to and including dismissal.

CONCLUSION

As such, it is quite clear from the above policies and procedures that the area of sex discrimination has increased in complexity considerably over recent years and continues to do so. Moreover, it is clear that the issue of the prohibition of discrimination touches on many aspects of the modern workplace in Ireland. What is also clear is that the burden and duty to protect Irish workers from discrimination, particularly sex discrimination, harassment and sexual harassment is increasingly placed, no longer on the member states and governments of the European Union but directly on employers themselves. This is most definitely the case in terms of Employment Equality Act 1998 in Ireland. Therefore, from its basic beginnings in the Treaty of Rome founding the European Economic Community in the 1950s, the principle of gender equality, that forms the cornerstone of the protection against sex discrimination in Ireland today, has developed and evolved to the extent that it touches aspects of our lives in social, economic and even constitutional terms that the Founders of the European Union could scarcely have realised. This is most recently seen in the case dealt with in this book of *KB v. National Health Service Pensions Agency and the Secretary of State for Health, European Court of Justice, January 7, 2004*, which has potentially far-reaching implications for every aspect of our legal system from family to constitutional to taxation law. Therefore, as the implications of such cases are teased out over future years, one thing is clear: such further developments protecting equality in Europe and, in particular, in Ireland are not only guaranteed but also very much far from complete.

Index